The General, The Boy, & Recapturing Joy
Inspiring Life Lessons from My Grandfather

The General, The Boy, & Recapturing Joy

Inspiring Life Lessons from My Grandfather

DR. BILL ATWOOD
© 2020

The General, The Boy, & Recapturing Joy
Inspiring Life Lessons From My Grandfather

© 2020 by Dr. Bill Atwood. All rights reserved.
ISBN 978-0-9913533-0-9

Cover design by Michael Holter. https/www.michaelholter.com All rights reserved.

Scripture taken from the New King James Version®. Copyright © 1982 by Thomas Nelson. Used by permission. All rights reserved.

No part of this publication may be reproduced in any form, including any means electronic, without the written permission of the author. The only exception is brief quotes in printed reviews.

Published in the United States of America

Ekklesia Society Publishing
P.O. Box 5343
Frisco, Texas 75035
800.303.6267

*This book is lovingly dedicated to my Grandfather,
Brigadier General James Arthur Pickering.
It is only in retrospect that I have begun to understand
the profound impact he had on my life,
and what a truly outstanding
mentor, grandfather, and man he was.*

Acknowledgements

I am deeply in debt to Marcus Warner, PhD, and Jim Wilder, PhD, for their help and encouragements in delving into what was a very new area of studying brain science. It is humbling to have a brain and have had so little understanding of how it works! Marcus and Jim, along with Chris and Jen Coursey, Amy Brown, and Ed and Maritza Khouri, have been wonderful and inspiring in helping me develop some understanding of neuroscience.

Major kudos to my gifted and patient editor, Lee Ligon-Borden, PhD, for countless hours spent on this text. Appreciation also to Barbara Ridge for proofreading assistance.

Table of Contents

Chapter 1	*The General – A Grandfather's Modeling and Teaching*	11
Chapter 2	*Designed for Joy – How We Are Meant to Live*	21
Chapter 3	*Designed for Joy – Level One – The Attachment Center*	26
Chapter 4	*Designed for Joy – Level Two- - The Assessment Center*	30
Chapter 5	*Designed for Joy – Level Three – The Attunement Center*	36
Dhapter 6	*Designed for Joy – Level Four – The Identity Center*	42
Chapter 7	*Designed for Joy – Level Five – Our Library*	47
Chapter 8	*Joy – What it Is and What it Isn't*	51
Chapter 9	*Recapturing Joy from* DESPAIR	57
Chapter 10	*Recapturing Joy from* SADNESS	65
Chapter 11	*Recapturing Joy from* ANGER	71
Chapter 12	*Recapturing Joy from* SHAME	79
Chapter 13	*Recapturing Joy from* DISGUST	85
Chapter 14	*Recapturing Joy from* FEAR	91
Chapter 15	*The Prefrontal Cortex – True Identity*	95
Chapter 16	*Acting Like My True Self in* DESPAIR	99
Chapter 17	*Acting Like My True Self in* SADNESS	103
Chapter 18	*Acting Like My True Self in* ANGER	107
Chapter 19	*Acting Like My True Self in* SHAME	111
Chapter 20	*Acting Like My True Self in* DISGUST	117
Chapter 21	*Acting Like My True Self in* FEAR	121
Chapter 22	*Connections & Community*	175
Scriptures for Those Times When Joy is Interrupted		131

Chapter 1
The General – A Grandfather's Modeling and Teaching

Brigadier General James Arthur Pickering

My earliest memory of all occurred when I was about two years old. I remember my Grandfather was carrying me around, and he was whispering in my ear, "Duty, Honor, Country," the motto of the United States Military Academy–West Point. I can remember hearing his quiet voice and having it settle into my soul as profoundly important–even life-defining.

His rough gray wool sweater rubbed against my cheek as I lay my head on his shoulder. His warm arms wrapped around me while we walked around. We were in the apartment where I lived with my mother and brother down the street from my Grandfather's house while my father was off fighting in Korea. As my Grandfather repeated "Duty, Honor, Country" over and over, I remember seeing a bright flash from the chrome on the washer and dryer in the laundry room, and the smell of the laundry soap and starch.

He continued to whisper those words, and I felt safe. Somehow, even as this message was being processed in my little two-year old mind and heart, I also felt commissioned. He was defining for me the core principles of life that would shape the direction I would later take. They also would judge the mistakes I would make, but the direction he declared over me certainly set my life's course.

My Grandfather, James Arthur Pickering, was a remarkable man. He was born on December 26, 1891, in Mendenhall, Mississippi. When he was twelve years old, his father died, leaving him, his mother, and his five siblings destitute. Being the eldest, he dropped out of school and went to work in a sawmill to support his family, until all his siblings finished school.

An avid reader, he somehow managed to get accepted into the University of Mississippi and attended for two years. His dream, however, was not a regular university. With the "gathering storm" in Europe, he was able to get a Presidential Appointment to West Point.

Besides having a distinct drive, he was also a man of deep humility. When he got a spot at The Point, despite having two years of college under his belt, he had to start all over as a Plebe, but he was willing to do that to achieve his dream. He regaled me with many stories of his time at "The Point," from teaching me the questions of Plebe Knowledge to singing "The Corps," and the song of the legendary publican (and Presbyterian churchman!) who surreptitiously served cadets adjacent to the West Point Campus, immortalized in the song "Benny Havens, Oh."

At four years old, I may have been the youngest child to master:

> How many lights in Cullum Hall?
> "340 lights, sir."
>
> How many gallons in Lusk Reservoir?
> "92.2 million gallons, sir, when the water is flowing over the spillway."

How many names on Battle Monument?
"2,240 names, sir."

How is the cow?
"Sir, she walks, she talks, she's full of chalk, the lacteal fluid extracted from the female of the bovine species is highly prolific to the nth degree."

What is the definition of leather?
"If the fresh skin of an animal, cleaned and divested of all hair, fat, and other extraneous matter, be immersed in a dilute solution of tannic acid, a chemical combination ensues; the gelatinous tissue of the skin is converted into a non-putrescible substance, impervious to and insoluble in water; this, sir, is leather."

I also reveled in being able to join along with recordings of the West Point Glee Club singing:

The Corps! The Corps! The Corps!

The Corps, bareheaded, salute it
With eyes up thanking our God That we of the Corps are treading, where they of the Corps have trod.

They are here in ghostly assemblage,
The men of the Corps long dead
And our hearts are standing attention,
While we wait for their passing tread.

We sons of today, we salute you
You Sons of an earlier day;
We follow, close order, behind you,
where you have pointed the way.

The long grey line of us stretches,
thro' the years of a century told
And the last man feels to his marrow
The grip of your far off hold.

Grip hands with us now, though we see not,
Grip hands with us strengthen our hearts.
As the long line stiffens and straightens
With the thrill that your presence imparts

Grip hands, tho' it be from the shadows
While we swear as you did of yore
Or living or dying to honor
The Corps, and The Corps, and The Corps.[1]

---

[1] https://www.youtube.com/watch?v=JkYSwnyJy70

Naturally, at two, and three, and four years of age, I didn't understand the implications, but I did know something important was happening. The fun—even silly—questions and answers and the solemn anthem "The Corps" wove a tapestry, imparting to me a sacred trust and the absolute certain truth that I had a destiny, and that destiny involved "Duty, Honor, Country."

United States Military Academy Class of 1916

My Grandfather finished his four years at West Point, graduating in 1916, and was immediately sent to Europe. It was so early in the life of the U.S. Army that his military serial number was O-4444. "O" for Officer and "4444" for the number of officers commissioned since starting service numbers. Initially, he was in the Horse Artillery and fought in the famous artillery battle at Chateau Thierry in France.

After World War I, he returned to the States and was tasked with taking his Horse Artillery Unit across Texas with ox-drawn carts, mules, and horses. Traveling a scant 15 miles a day (the limit an ox could cover!), he trekked from San Antonio toward Del Rio (where I would later attend USAF Pilot training).

Along the journey, he was kicked in the head by a mule and lost an eye. Ordinarily, that injury would have resulted in immediate expulsion from the U.S. Army, but his service had attracted such attention that a special bill was introduced in the United States Congress to allow him to continue on Active Duty with only one eye!

He rose through the ranks and eventually became a Brigadier General. During World War II, he became the Commanding General , Division Artillery, of the 8th Infantry Division. While leading that unit, he was awarded a Silver Star "for conspicuous gallantry and intrepidity in connection with military operations against the enemy." One can only imagine how rare it was for a General Officer to receive a Silver Star, the third highest award for valor. The three highest medals recognizing valor are the Medal of Honor, the Distinguished Service Cross (DSC), followed by the Silver Star.

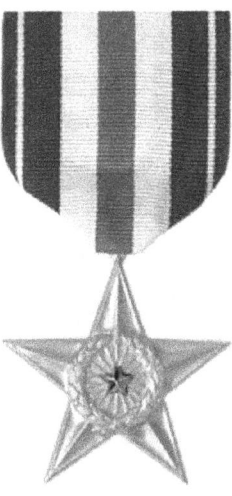

Eventually, my Grandfather became, first, the Chief-of-Intelligence and, later, the Chief-of-Staff for General George Patton and served at the Battle of the Bulge.

After World War II, he was stationed at Fort MacPherson in Atlanta, Georgia, and retired from the 3rd Army there. It worked out perfectly, so he could be with me every day when I was very young and my father was away for almost five years, fighting in Korea.

My Grandfather somehow got the nickname "Daddy Pick," as he served the fatherhood role while my father was gone. He was every inch a father to me. As Daddy Pick taught me about duty; he also taught me many other valuable lessons. One might expect him to have been a severe man, having seen the horrors of World War I and II. Often, I would see him looking off to the horizon, remembering, but when he saw me, he would quickly recover and be utterly present. He was willing to tell me that there were many hard things he had endured, but he never gave details. One important lesson was that when he shared about something negative or difficult, he always framed it in the midst of something positive. The "something positive" would usually be based on his prime motivations: *Duty, Honor, and Country.*

My Grandfather's house on Alpine Road, Atlanta

I loved his old house on Alpine Road in Atlanta, especially his workshop. It had wonder upon wonder for a small boy. I loved the smell and the tools, and I relished the way he would slowly explain how to use each tool.

"Look, son," he would say. "If you turn the chisel this way, the edge forces it to cut deeper with each hit.

"Turn it over and you can cut off the thinnest sliver of wood. Here, where we are setting a hinge on this door, we need a shallow cut. When we make the opening for the door latch, we'll cut deep enough for the latch to go in."

Often, he would pat the bench on which he sat, calling me to sit. "Look," he would say, sweeping his arm in an arc pointing to the tools in racks on the wall. "All these tools will be yours one day. No one else appreciates them or knows how to use them for that matter! Before we're done, I'll show you how to use the wood plane, and the brace and bit. With the right knowledge and the right tools, you can be a master of wood and make it whatever you want or need it to be."

Sometimes, he would tell me wonderful stories with a crooked smile. One of those was about his trek across Texas with the horse artillery and the ox carts. When they eventually got to Del Rio on the banks of the Rio Grande River, there was an Army Fort a few miles from town. The area was so dry that the Army actually introduced camels to deal with the desert-like atmosphere. Every evening at sunset, the troops would fire a cannon and lower the flag at the Army Post. The next day, the Quartermaster of the Army Post would ride into town and set his clock to the master clock at the railroad station.

Eventually, someone coming to Del Rio found that the Army and railroad clocks were about thirty minutes different from the pocket watch that the visitor carried.

"How do you suppose that happened?" asked my Grandfather. "They didn't know and couldn't understand it, but eventually figured out what was happening. Each night at 5:00 pm, the canon would fire, and the flag would be lowered. The next day, the quartermaster would go into town and set his watch to the Railroad Station clock. The quartermaster's clock would strike 5:00 pm the next day, the canon would fire, and the flag would be lowered. What they found was that the stationmaster was setting his clock to the sound of the canon firing several miles away at the Army Post, thinking that was exactly 5:00 o'clock. It took quite a few seconds for the sound to get to the rail station where the station master would update his clock. But it wasn't actually 5:00 o'clock, it was just a little after 5:00. The difference wasn't a lot, but over the months and years, the few seconds delay from the sound of the cannon firing being heard in town added up to the clock eventually being a half-hour late! The lesson," he said with a grin, "is you have to be sure that the star you are using for navigation is a good one!"

And we would laugh.

Of all his lessons for me, one of the most important was how to remain calm and to quiet myself in the midst of tension—even in the midst of battle. He would say, "If we perish while doing good, it is enough that we did what is right; and posterity will be kind to us. Pouring out our lives in the service of our country, battling evil, is a worthwhile endeavor."

In various circumstances, he would draw me close and sit me on his lap. I can remember the stiff cloth of his old uniform shirts. Though he removed the insignia, he was so used to them from a lifetime of wearing uniforms, he would often default to wearing the old shirts around the house. He would hold me—often tightly—and be very still with quiet, slow breathing and help me to calm my heart.

> *From the General:*
> If we perish while doing good, it is enough that we did what is right; and posterity will be kind to us. Pouring out our lives in the service of our country while battling evil is a worthwhile endeavor.
> -- Brig. Gen. James A. Pickering

Regardless of how upset I was, entering into that quiet and safe place in his arms and on his lap, I would quickly be able to calm my heart and be still, having confidence that life was good. I didn't know it, but he was teaching me and helping me to learn to work through a variety of unsettling emotions that were robbing me of peace. Over the years, I have actually been rather amazed that everyone else didn't have the skills to quiet themselves, but then I've come to notice that many people don't have an internal compass guiding them either. Both of those were great gifts from my Grandfather.

My ability to quiet myself ebbed and flowed over the years. When negative things happened, at first, circumstances could be devastating. My Grandfather had shown me, however, that it is possible to return to joy and know peace, even in adverse circumstances. Even though I often would be discombobulated, I eventually would settle down, even if it took some time. That ability was true, even in the midst of some really challenging circumstances. Often, in those times, I would think of him, such as taking a drink when thirsty, and find myself quieting and returning to joy.

Years later, as I heard teaching from Ed Khouri, Jim Wilder, Chris and Jen Coursey, and Marcus Warner, I began to discover that quieting, returning to joy, and having the reserves to act like my true self, were "things" that could be nurtured to enrich our lives.

While reading and listening to the Brain Science teachers, I learned that we should be able to return to joy from any of the six major negative emotions – in something like 90 seconds! It has taken a while, but I've found that applying the techniques I've learned in studying how the brain works, along with the foundational guidance from my Grandfather, that it is usually possible to recapture joy quickly. There is more about this in the chapters that follow!

We were created for joy. Jesus said it, and we long for it. God's design is that our thoughts and hearts would be joyful, and our relationships are designed to increase our capacity to experience joy.

Because of sin, and the consequences of The Fall, many things in life do not bring joy. The chapters that follow relate instances when I have been greatly upset and describe how I have learned to recapture the joy that God wants me to have.

Eventually, we will be with the Lord in heaven, where our joy will be full. Until then, we need to learn how to recapture joy when we are assaulted by situations that are upsetting. First, though, before we talk about returning to joy, let's look at how our brain works to build joy, and how we are designed to live in joy and act as our intended selves.

Chapter 2
Designed for Joy
How We Are Meant to Live

As we glance back to creation, we see God's wonderful purpose to create people to live with Him in joy. In Heaven before the Fall, all there was to be found was joy. This creation mirrors the perfect fellowship of the Trinity and the angelic festivity focused on the worship of God. In the midst of this glorious worship, a corruption arose when the archangel, Lucifer, rebelled. God cast him from heaven, along with approximately one-third of the angels. With the traitors expelled, joyful worship continued, but trouble was brewing on the earth.

In the Garden, God's created beings dwelt in an environment ideal for experiencing joy with God and one another. This perfect home became the target of the fallen Lucifer's wrath. Still at enmity with God, Lucifer led Adam and Eve into sin. Joy was devastated; instead, death reigned (Romans 5:14).

To remedy our fallen state, Jesus endured crucifixion, burial, and resurrection, securing our redemption and wonderfully redeeming everything to restore God's original design. People have all sinned, and we desperately need redemption. Scripture clearly shows that Jesus is the only one who can provide the pathway to this abundant life. It all happens in a way that brings even greater glory to God:

> *My Father is glorified by this, that you bear much fruit and become my disciples. As the Father has loved me, so I have loved you; abide in my love. If you keep my commandments, you will abide in my love, just as I have kept my Father's commandments and abide in his love. I have said these things to you so that my joy may be in you, and that your joy may be complete. (John 15:8-11)*

Although that joy was assaulted in The Fall, the redemption wrought by Jesus Christ will lead us to live in joy again in heaven. Until then, we can recapture joy by being in a relationship with Him and learning how to return to joy when we are assaulted by negative emotions.

In the last few years, I've begun to learn something about how the brain works and about the impact that its inner workings have on relationships and ministry. Some of the wonderful resources that have given me insights are found:

>   ThriveToday.org
>   DeeperWalkInternational.org
>   LifeModelWorks.org

In these ministries, people such as Jim and Kitty Wilder, Dr. Karl Lehman, Marcus Warner, Amy Brown, Chris and Jen Coursey, Andrew Miller, Dr. Curt Thompson, Dr. Dan Siegel, and others have shared the fruits of their research, rendering information on how the brain works more accessible to us.

Before we discuss how to "recapture joy," I'd like to share some recent discoveries in brain science. Your brain really is an amazing organ — the product of God's intricate design, and that design is to live in joy.

In the 1970s, magnetic resonance imaging developed into a powerful tool for three-dimensional mapping of the human body. By the late 1980s, a new dynamic application came into play when researchers used two MRIs simultaneously to assess brain activation between a pair interacting volunteers. Amazingly, the discovery revealed how an individual's action stimulated a distinct area in their own brain, as well as the identical location in the brain of the fellow volunteer.

In *The Developing Mind,* Dr. Dan Siegel points out that most people think of the brain as purely "cranial" (in the head), but in reality, it is "somatic,"[2] (*soma* in Greek means *body*) because the entire nervous system is connected to the brain. Every nerve in the fingertips and toes is connected to the brain, just as much as the "mental" things that we usually think about.

Sensory information from the body is used by the brain to assess how things are going. Dr. Siegel writes, "The brain looks to the body to know how it feels and to assess the meaning of things..."[3]

It is crucial to learn to become aware of our body's sensations so we can process things as they actually are. Of course, how we feel is not always how one *should* feel ideally, but if we can't assess how we actually feel and don't know where we are, it is all but impossible for us to navigate to

---

[2] Siegel, Daniel. (2012) *The Developing Mind: How Relationships and the Brain Interact to Shape Who We Are.* New York: The Guilford Press.

[3] Siegel, Daniel. (2001) *Parenting from the Inside Out.* New York, NY: The Guilford Press, p. 189.

where we *should* be. A person's thinking can get stuck in the lower levels of the brain (called the *limbic region*), a condition some scientists describe as living in our "reptile brain." I suppose that is because reptiles, which do not share higher cognitive functions, share the lower-level brain parts with us. One of my friends calls his lower level responses to some crises as living in his "lizard brain." He goes on to say that being stuck in the lower levels of the brain does not lead to his acting as his most noble self!

Speaking of neuroscience, Dr. Siegel goes on to say, "...you may be surprised to learn how much it teaches us about the interconnection of our minds—both individually and within our larger community."[4] But, as the late-night commercials say, "There's more!"

When I read Dr. Siegel's observations, I was struck by the thought that the brain is like having a wireless, or WIFI, connection, whereby one person can connect with another, with neurological information passing across the physical divide between them, by using smell, voice, and eye contact. Of course, touch can be involved as well. When we "connect" brains, it is called *attunement, syncing*, or some authors call it a *mutual mind state*. It's not that everything is shared, but it is remarkable that some things *are*!

How it Works: The Make-up of the Brain

Many people go through life taking all their thoughts, actions, and experiences for granted, with no consideration about that organ seated between their ears. Yet, the brain is extremely complex, and although my expertise is really limited, here is an attempt to describe some of what goes on.

First of all, the brain is divided into two parts, called *hemispheres* (right and left), which in some ways mirror each other but in other ways have profound differences. The left hemisphere deals in naming things, processing facts, and making decisions. The right hemisphere operates in terms of pictures and relationships.[5] We can be aware of our thoughts in the left hemisphere because we are conscious of what we are thinking. We are not able to monitor the right hemisphere directly because it operates at a faster number of cycles per second than does the logical left side of the brain; also, it is doing things about which we are not *consciously* aware. Despite being outside our conscious thoughts, these

---

[4] *Ibid.*, Preface
[5] *Ibid.*, Introduction

activities are powerful. Although the actions of the right hemisphere are hidden from our intellectual observation, they are not completely inaccessible.

Experiences are processed in the right hemisphere in a series of steps, rather than all at once, in what neuro-theologian Dr. Jim Wilder describes as four "levels" of the brain.[6] As experiences are processed and work their way through the pathways in our right hemisphere, a worldview is constructed and presented to our left hemisphere. That worldview, in turn, becomes the context in which we live and make decisions. It is extremely powerful and articulates "Who am I, who are my people, and how do we act in this set of circumstances?"

Unfortunately, often experiences in relationships do not create accurate worldviews to be communicated to the left hemisphere; rather, the worldviews are skewed or warped, and decisions are made accordingly, often to the detriment of everyone involved. This is how excitement is generated by novels or movies that have what we call an "omniscient" narrator, who allows the audience to know things about which the characters know nothing, or have wrong perspectives, and we witness the faulty decisions they make based on their limited worldviews. Romeo and Juliet are prime examples. In life also, these faulty worldviews can have devastating consequences.

It's important, then, to look first at how experiences are processed through the pathways of the right hemisphere of the brain in what Dr. Wilder describes as the four "levels."

It is very helpful to know what is supposed to happen, relationally speaking. When we know what is supposed to happen in the development of healthy relationships, we can identify what is missing or has been detrimental, or celebrate what has worked well.

We will look now at Levels of Process in the Right Hemisphere.

---

[6] Wilder, Jim. (2004) *The Complete Guide to Living with Men*. Pasadena: Shepherd's House, p. 39.

Chapter 3
Designed for Joy

Level One - The Attachment Center
The Thalamus and the Nucleus Accumbens

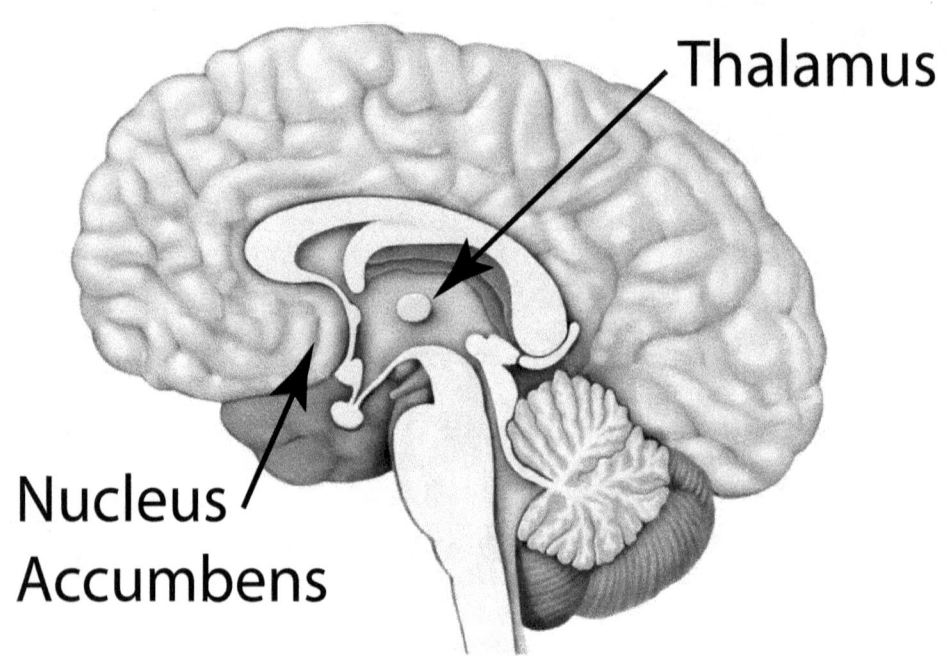

The first level of the brain is called "Level One." It is composed of two components: the **thalamus** and the **basal ganglia** (which includes the **nucleus accumbens**). Together, they form the "Attachment Center." These parts of the right hemisphere are constantly monitoring stimuli around us to decide what is relevant. We "attach" to those things and ignore others. They poll the senses in the body in order to make an assessment that can be passed on to "Level Two," for evaluation.

This Level One "Attachment Center" is where our deepest relational attachments take place. Some of the attachment is profound, such as the links we are supposed to form with our mother and father. If that attachment is missing or damaged, it creates a terrible problem, called an *attachment wound*. An attachment wound involves being attached to something that is not helpful or not having attachment to someone with whom we should be connected. Information that is passed on to other areas of the brain from this Level One will be tainted in the event of an attachment wound.

Our first attachment is with our mother. From her, we are supposed to learn the permanence of love and discover the joy that comes from relationships. With a healthy mother's love in our lives, we experience security that helps carry us through life.

> *A young man I knew named Tim had AIDS. Because of the immunodeficiency, he had contracted pneumocystic pneumonia, a very painful and frightening form of pneumonia that was inhibiting his breathing. It was an extremely distressing time for him. He knew he was dying and was wracked with pain. He was afraid of how God would judge him and was afraid of what would happen when he died.*
>
> *I tried many ways to minister to him as his pastor. The only thing that gave him relief was when I held him in my arms late into the night, and rocked him while I talked with him, sang, or prayed for him. This experience takes on new meaning now that I have learned more about how the brain works. Because Tim had experienced bonding with his mother when he was very young, he was able to form a bonding connection with me as I rocked him that gave him relief. When I held him, his positive memories of being loved as a child were transferred to the pains of the present and gave him solace. In this case, the relationship that he had experienced with his mother years previously*

> *provided an open door for positive ministry in this challenging time of his life.*

Contrariwise, wounds at this level can result in the most intense and awful pain.[7] Although the wound occurs at Level One, the brain actually manifests the pain at a higher level, the Cingulate Cortex (which we will get to in a moment). MRI research shows that emotional pain manifests in the brain very similarly to physical pain.[8]

This level of the brain where connections begin includes the thalamus and the nucleus accumbens. Whereas the thalamus makes the relational connections, the nucleus accumbens is the center for pain and pleasure. The nucleus accumbens will "code" a connection being made by the thalamus, associating it with pain or pleasure. It also creates a craving for attachment. In unhealthy situations, addictive behavior can result as an attempt to substitute something else for the attachment we really need When the thalamus and nucleus accumbens are doing their work, the collected stimuli are sent upstream in the brain, much like a railcar being loaded to be sent to the next station for assessment.

It is also at the attachment level that the desire to connect with someone else is born. It can be expressed as a desire to talk, hug, listen, or grow in joy. When we sense that urging, it is called having our "attachment light" on, as we long to connect significantly with someone else. Ultimately, our deepest longing for attachment is to come into an intimate relationship with God.

When the need for linking is not met, the result can be very distressing, ranging from discomfort to a deep primal pain of abandonment. Those who remain insecure in their ability to attach with others experience deep pain, not only remembering what was lacking in their childhoods, but having that pain resurface in other circumstances as well.[9] In fact, it can be pervasive in their lives.

Demonstrating this, in the opening line of *Anna Karenina*, Leo Tolstoy sees joy as a common currency of healthy families, recognizing many families are not happy. "All happy families resemble one another, but each

---

[7] Jaffe, Eric. (2013) *Why Love Literally Hurts*, Association for Psychological Science, Observer.

[8] *Ibid.*

[9] Davies KA, Macfarlane GJ, McBeth J, Morriss R, and Dickens C. (2009) *Insecure attachment style is associated with chronic widespread pain.* Pain. 143(3-24): 200-205.

unhappy family is unhappy in its own way."[10] So too, Christians may know this common currency of joy. When Jesus said, "… that your joy may be complete" (John 5:11), He was indicating to us that He has completely overcome the effects of the Fall and is establishing a new order, and that is one of joy. As Christians, we take the Word of Jesus Christ to be authoritative—and that should be so, even when circumstances try to dissuade us. We may be going through a rough patch or may be experiencing something acutely painful. The circumstances may shout to us that all is lost, but we are called to cling to the promise that Jesus came in order to bring us to joy precisely in those painful circumstances.

---

[10] Tolstoy, Leo. (1873, 1877) *Anna Karenina*. Reissue 2017, MacMillan Collector's Library, London: Pan MacMillan, London, p. 1.

Chapter 4
Designed for Joy

Level Two - The Assessment Center
The Amaygdala

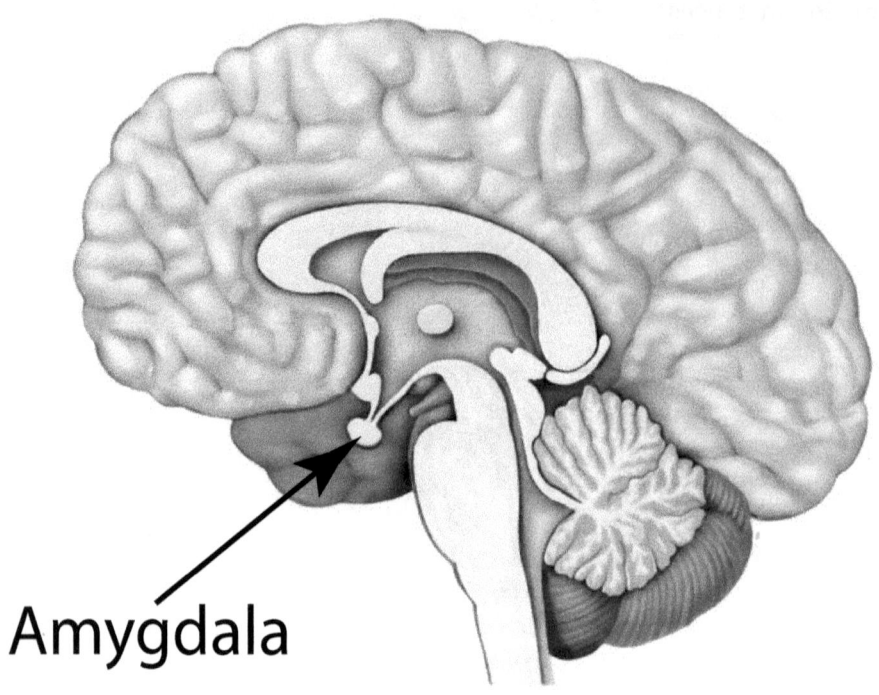

Amygdala

From the thalamus, the trainload of information is sent to the next station, the "Assessment Center," called the **amygdala**. The amygdala's job is to label the things that are presented to it as being good, bad, or frightening. The cells of the nucleus accumbens "receive input from the amygdaloid complex ...from the hippocampal formation...and from cells of the bed nucleus of the stria terminalis."[11] All that means is that the nucleus accumbens and amygdala are linked together to help us decide about the stimuli around us. For our purposes here, it is the wiring to the amygdala that is the most important. The nucleus accumbens sends out signals to the senses to get input to help in deciding whether something is good, bad, or scary.

The brain chemically records this assessment permanently, forming new neural pathways. You can read more about how new neural pathways develop in *The Developing Mind*, by Dr. Dan Siegel.[12] The neural pathways are bathed in different chemicals depending on how the amygdala "encodes" them. I envision this as being like spray painting the path with different colors. Later on, as the Pre-Frontal Cortex looks back, it is like the "good" pathways are painted green, and the brain identifies that path as building the identity of who I am and who my people are. When I have a collection of "good" experiences, I will look on those as I build my understanding of my "tribe."

As the amygdala is making its judgment, it is very helpful if the assessment is an accurate one, as a faulty judgment can pose significant issues. For example, something that is *bad* can be recorded as *good*. That faulty construct will play out dangerously because we will not have judgment to protect ourselves from the danger of the bad thing, and we will embrace it uncritically. We see this frequently in individuals who go from one abusive relationship to another, thinking the fault in the relationship lies with them, rather than the abusers. Having experienced abuse as a child, one may record those actions as appropriate and actually seek out that behavior in their adult relationships because it feels normal, even "comfortable." Because abuse can be very subtle (e.g., the parent who demands perfection), it can be difficult to identify and, in turn, to gain a correct perspective.

---

[11] Willis MA, Haines DE. (2018) Chapter 31. The Limbic System, in *Fundamental Neuroscience for Basic and Clinical Applications (Fifth Edition)*. Philadelphia: Elsevier, Inc., p. 457.
[12] Siegel, *The Developing Mind. op. cit.*

On the other hand, if something is *good* but the circumstances in our lives and environment cause us to record it as *bad*, we may miss out on blessings that God intends for us to have. I am reminded of a woman we will call Mary.

> From the time she was a child, Mary was reminded by her mother, a person who is expected to provide positive input, of the time that her father "wasted" money on her by buying her two $25 dresses (this was in the 1940s, so they were quite expensive dresses) when she was only two years old. The message Mary recorded was that she was not worth that expense. Other input from her mother reinforced that misguided assessment. Not until God healed her of that false perspective did she begin to understand a father's love and, consequently, her heavenly Father's love. One day as she was driving and remembering the story for the millionth time, a voice in her head said, "Your FATHER thought you were worth two $25 dresses." Suddenly, she realized how warped her mother's perspective was and that her father had lavished love, not extravagance, on her. She realized that her heavenly Father wanted to do the same. Her entire worldview and relationship with God changed in that moment.

When we encounter actual frightening events or people, it is helpful for that assessment to be recorded in our amygdala-driven memory bank to protect us from harm in the future. Not all things we experience as frightening are actually dangerous, however, and problems can arise when we label things as scary when they shouldn't be. An interesting example is the Vox poll of 1,999 people that showed really surprising numbers of Americans polled had some level of coulrophobia (fear of clowns).[13]

The chart on the next page reveals that a lot of people assessed clowns as being frightening at some point in their lives, as recorded in the amygdala. Hence, from thenceforth their initial reaction to encountering a clown is, "That is scary." Every subsequent time they encounter a clown, their first reaction is fear, when in fact the clowns pose no danger. It is interesting that many children's lullabies or stories present frightening experiences – the baby in the tree top falls to the ground,

---

[13] https://www.vox.com/2016/10/21/13321536/clown-scare-sightings-2016

cradle and all; Bambi's mother is killed, leaving Bambi alone; Hansel and Gretel are put in an oven by a wicked witch!

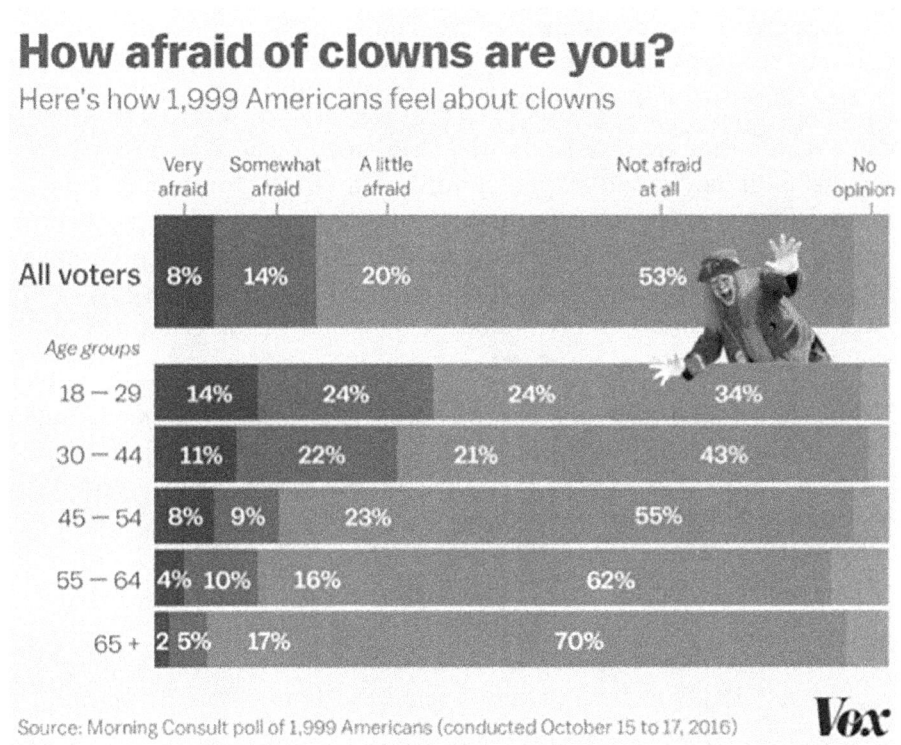

This chart reveals that a lot of people assessed clowns as being frightening at some point in their lives, as recorded in the amygdala. Hence, from thenceforth their initial reaction to encountering a clown is, "That is scary." Every subsequent time they encounter a clown, their first reaction is fear, when in fact the clowns pose no danger.

We'll look later at how to give new information to our right hemisphere. For now, I hope it is helpful to know there is a life "workaround" to the permanent labels the amygdala puts out.

Andrew Miller describes this level of the brain/mind as "The Guardian."[14] Not only can The Guardian send assessments up to level three, it can also send a message directly to our left hemisphere area of "fight or flight." When we encounter someone with great defenses up, we may actually be encountering their Guardians protecting them. In conversations, often you can identify The Guardian at work. When the person is speaking in defensive, protective terms, he or she likely is experiencing some perceived danger.

Adjacent to the amygdala is the hippocampus. The hippocampus interacts (still beyond our perception) with the information from the amygdala to process learning and emotions to brand things further. I envision it as being the Dymo© label-maker of the brain, labeling experiences that pass by for further review. The hippocampus also processes smell and sound memories and attaches emotions to the decisions that have been recorded.

> When I was a young boy in school, we lived in Germany. During the day, students would be sent to the Army dentist, who had an office down the hall in the school. Sadly, those dentists did not use any pain killers. I had a great deal of work that was done without any novocaine. In fact, I never even heard of novocaine until I was 15 years old. You can well imagine that I have a very strongly held attitude that dentists are bad and scary! You can well imagine the anxiety level I experienced every time I had to go to a dentist. I managed to do it, but it was a terrible experience every time.
>
> It was only years later as an adult that I went to a dentist and said, "OK, here's the deal. If you hurt me, I won't pay you!" The dentist laughed. I said, "I'm not kidding."
>
> He paused and then said, "OK. I can live with that."

Since then, I have had a good deal of dental work done, but it has not been painful! He has lived up to the deal.

Even with the expert care of my good dentist, when I hear the whining sound of the drill, it sends a shudder through me. This happens even though the current dentist has never hurt me. The association of the

---

[14] Miller, Andrew. (2018) HeartSync Basic Seminar (Rev Edition). FL: Self-Published. Contact P.O. Box 14186, Tallahassee, Florida 32317. - available at: http://www.heartsyncministries.org

sound of the drill prompts a strong response. It takes a great deal of discipline to stay put and try to relax so he can do his work.

This is the logical left hemisphere saying, "Ok, guys, we have some new information. We can make it through this!" Nonetheless, my first primal response to the sound of the drill is, "Flee!"

Chapter 5
Designed for Joy

Level Three - The Attunement Center
The Cingulate Cortex

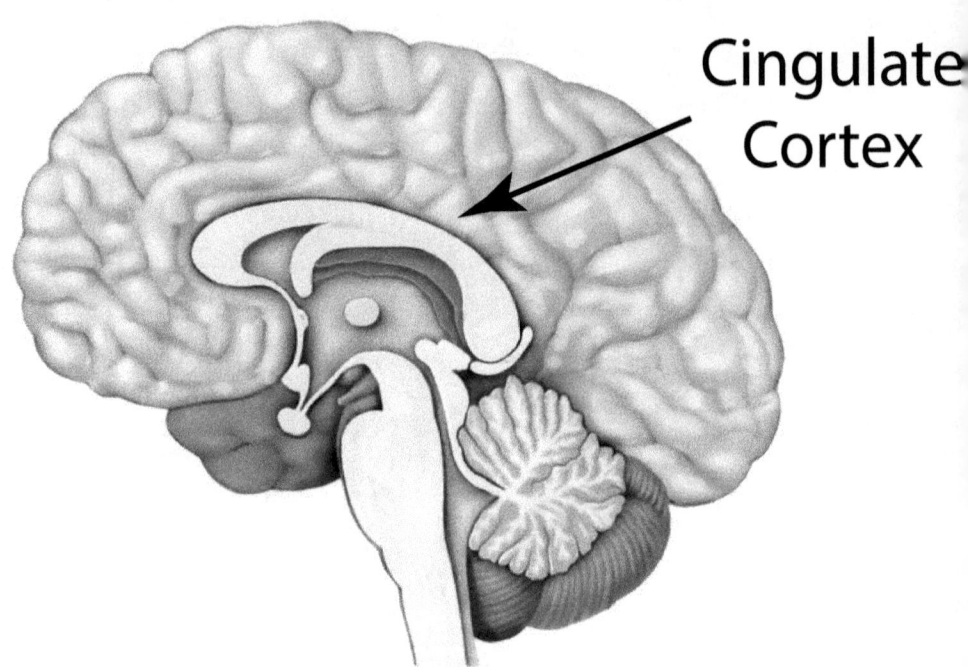

The third level of the right hemisphere is called the **cingulate cortex**. It is a banana-shaped part of the brain. Its function is to relate with the cingulate cortex in other people's brains to provide a connection that is called *attunement*. In their book, *RARE Leadership*, Jim Wilder and Marcus Warner describe the purpose of the cingulate cortex: it "reads" people and synchronizes with their feelings."[15]

The cingulate cortex is the part of the brain where many emotions are experienced. It is also the place where we link with other people. In Heartsync, Andrew Miller simply calls this part of our brain "Emotion."

Everyone probably knows about people with whom they "click" and have a really good relationship, right from the beginning. Some of that relational "clicking" is actually the connecting of the cingulate cortex of one person to that same part of another person's brain. It is in this portion of the brain that we have a two-way connection, which can make something like six round trips of information from our brain to someone else's every second.

That connection, sometimes called a *mutual mind state*, is also called *attunement*. It is the state in which our connection is not only based on joy, but also increases the joyful connection. As we live in joy with another person, the relationship gets increasingly better, and the brain records more joy. The more we live in joy, the easier it is to remain in joy, and we build more momentum toward joy.

Attunement occurs when we (and another person) are open to relational contacts and are "connected." Twinned with our relational circuits being on is the urging of our attachment light to be on. For connections to take place, we must intentionally prepare ourselves to be in relationship with others.

Relational circuits also can be turned *off* or simply *not activated*; indications of having relational circuits off are:
- Wanting to get away
- Not being interested in the other person
- Being distracted
- Not caring about the other person

---

[15] Warner M, Wilder J. (2016) *Rare Leadership: 4 Uncommon Habits for Increasing Trust, Joy, and Engagement in the People You Lead*. Chicago: Moody Publishers, p. 67.

- Considering others as a distraction or nuisance
- Preferring to focus on tasks rather than people

Even though relational circuits are part of our brains and would normally be considered intangible, some *physical* things we do can turn on our relational circuits. That action is possible because the nervous system provides an interface among our thoughts, our subconscious, and our physical selves.

One nerve in particular serves as an interface between our bodies and the cingulate cortex (where relationship connections occur): the vagus nerve, the stimulation of which causes our brain to open relational circuits and helps us prepare to connect with others. The vagus nerve is so called because it is the Latin word for *wandering*. It gets that name because the vagus nerve "wanders" from the brain to various organs in the chest, abdomen, and neck, and even our gut.

Stimulating the vagus nerve activates the cells in the cingulate cortex to prepare to interact with others. That stimulation can be achieved by several means. One way is by alternating rubbing and tapping the spots where the vagus nerve comes close to the surface of our skin just above our pectoral muscles. You can stimulate the nerve by tapping those spots while slowly breathing in and out, and rubbing in small circles as you breathe out.

There are other ways to indirectly stimulate the vagus nerve. One is by yawning slowly to the left and right. That opens our relational circuits as well, by stimulating the cingulate cortex. There are other exercises with breathing and specific facial expressions of surprise, while we raise our open hands like a surprised child would do.

An easier method is to express appreciation verbally. When we speak affirmations of gratitude, the part of our brain that is activated is the same part that is activated when we are in a relationship. Five minutes of expressing appreciation for a variety of things will turn our relational circuits on and help us prepare to connect with others.

If two people both have their relational circuits on and their attachment lights on with each other, their brains begin to sync. As one shares emotions, body sensations, and verbal information, the brain of the listener begins to "light up" in the very same areas as those of the speaker's brain. Sharing emotions and physical sensations provides the brain the signals needed to connect. The connection is perceived as a positive experience, and joy develops.

The Joy Smile

Another great tool in this process of connecting with someone else is what is called a *joy smile*. It involves simply making eye contact, usually emphasizing the other person's left eye because it is wired to the right hemisphere of that person's brain. As we spend time with joy smiles, new "white matter" is created in our brains and that of the other person with whom we are sharing. It may sound hokey, but I can tell you from experience that the fruit of joy smiles is an enriched relationship. Doing a joy smile with my wife Susan is profoundly wonderful.

The attunement center of the brain also has the role of deciding how much energy I want to put into a specific relationship. All relationships are not meant to exist at the same level of intimacy. With a spouse, of course, we will have a much deeper level of intimacy and connection than we would have with a casual friend. Some relationships may be positive but very temporary, as those we have, for example, with a grocery store clerk. It is fine to connect nicely while we are paying for groceries, but it is not reasonable to expect that we will develop a deep, finely attuned permanent relationship with them.

Because attunement takes place in the cingulate cortex, it is described as "cortical." It is the deepest level at which we have awareness.[16] Although it is very subtle, as we pay attention to attuning with others, we can sense that joy is developing. In the ministry HeartSync, this level is called "The Dancer,"[17] because dancing is often engaged with a partner. This level is designed to enjoy connecting with others and building joy.

Joy-Quiet Rhythm

Twinned with joy connections must also be times of quiet. A baby may love to be tickled but only for a short time. If the tickling continues non-stop, that which was a source of joy begins to be a source of torment. In healthy relationships, we learn to have a joy-quiet rhythm. With joy smiles, this could be a period of time—say a minute of eye contact, followed by a time—maybe fifteen or twenty seconds--when eye contact is broken and a quiet refreshing occurs. When this skill is a new experience, the time period during which the joy smile is comforting may last only a few seconds before we need to break eye contact. As we develop more facility with joy smiles, our capacity will be increased, and

---

[16] Adapted from the Life Model http://www.lifemodel.org/wordhtml/cc1.htm [17] Miller, *HeartSync, op. cit.*

we will be able to maintain joyful contact for longer periods of time before we need a break.

When I am doing joy smiles, I imagine a cup that is slowly filling up. When it fills, then we feel like it is time to look away and have some moments of rest. When we sense we are replete, we avert our eye contact.

After a pause, the joy smiles can resume. Repeating this cycle is actually surprisingly delightful. Before long, it becomes profoundly fruitful. With my wife, it has become something that we pursue to recharge, enjoy, and celebrate. I was very surprised how profound it has been. Joy smiles have enriched our marriage tremendously.

Quieting

Quieting is the skill we must learn to still our thoughts and still our bodies. Both body and mind can be caught up in crises and tensions. I find that a good way to begin to quiet is to begin to relax my muscles starting at the bottom of my feet. With eyes closed in a comfortable chair, I imagine relaxing my feet, then ankles, calves, thighs, abdomen, and so forth. If I am getting distracted, I will focus on one of the parts that needs to still and relax until it is.

Once quieting begins in my body, then I focus on a place in my mind in which I have a memory of an encouraging time with Jesus. For me, I often go back to a time in prayer when I perceived the face of Jesus as the face of Aslan the Lion from the *Chronicles of Narnia*.[18] I can easily imagine Him drawing close and leaning His forehead against mine. It is the most peaceful thing I have ever experienced. Going back to that place in my mind brings a flood of peace. If distractions intrude, I will acknowledge them and mentally sweep them aside with a wave of my hand, like I am gently pushing them to the side. I have found that it does not work to try to "push down" those kinds of thoughts. They need to be acknowledged and ushered aside.

---

[18] Lewis, CS. (1978) *The Chronicles of Narnia. Book Two: The Lion, The Witch and the Wardrobe.* NY: Harper Collins, p. 126.

Chapter 6
Designed for Joy

Level Four - The Identity Center
The Prefrontal Cortex

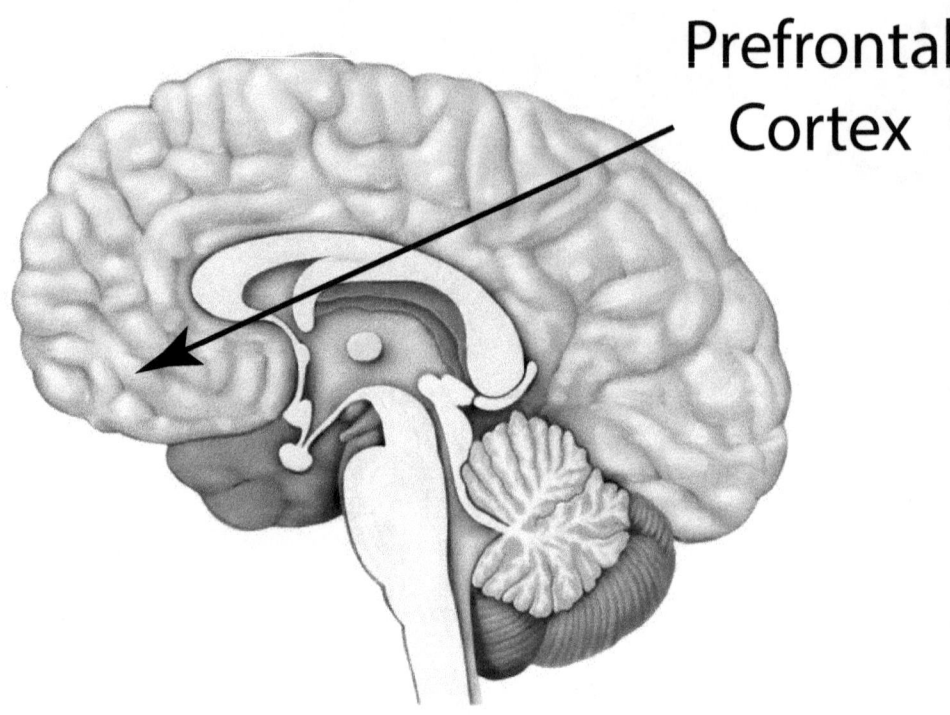

The largest part of the brain is the prefrontal cortex (**PFC**). There is one PFC on the right hemisphere and one on the left, which HeartSync calls "The Professor."[19] In the right hemisphere, the purpose of the PFC is to address three questions:

1. Who am I, Lord?
2. Who are my people?
3. How do we act in this certain circumstance?

Imagine what happens if at any of the levels leading up to the PFC, broken or faulty information occurs and is passed up the line. When the information is presented to the PFC, it constructs a subconscious system that informs our beliefs in the left hemisphere PFC. That which is constructed may be faulty, but we will be unaware of the problem because the process occurs subconsciously, and *seems* to us to be "true." Not being cognitively aware of this construction, we will think that our warped subconscious understanding is accurate. Faulty though it is, we will consider it to be axiomatic and as unchangeable as gravity. Of course, the huge problem is that we often make decisions based on what we are certain is true but is not. The great American humorist, Josh Billings, said, "It ain't so much people's ignorance that does the harm as their knowing so darned much that ain't so."[20]

When we go through negative experiences in which we feel that we are alone, the experience is recorded in our brains as

Note on Brain Science

Recent research indicates that the chemical response to neglectful, absent, or abusive parenting may trigger the excessive release of a chemical called "Substance P."[1]

Substance P is a cocktail of chemicals that for a long time has been associated with gastrointestinal inflammation and other diseases. (Though its presence has positive impact on muscle control.)[1]

There are indications that this chemical impacts not only the central nervous system, but it also impacts other areas of the brain.[1]

It is not fully understood how it functions, but it also seems to impact somehow cause a permanent record of negative times of abuse.

---

[19] Miller, *HeartSync*, op. cit.
[20] Billings, Josh. *The Country Gentleman*, (Attributed in *The Atlantic Monthly, Cambridge*, The Riverside Press, Volume CXII, p. 140).

trauma, and research indicates the release of a chemical called *Substance P* occurs (see sidebar). We don't need to learn how the release of this chemical works specifically in the brain, but it is useful to know that the process of recording events and interpreting them is a physical, neurological process. When there are wounds and traumas, understanding that things have been recorded physically may help understand why it is inadequate to tell people to "simply snap out of it" when they are in distress.

Thank God, wounds and traumas can be revisited with Jesus, and He can bring healing to us.

Long after we have experienced an original emotional pain, similar or related circumstances can cause us to re-experience the pain of the original trauma, probably without realizing that the "trigger" is not caused by the current circumstances but instead by the embedded memory. Dr. Siegel points out that when we experience something similar to an earlier trauma, it feels like we are experiencing pain in the current moment, but what is actually occurring is that we are "triggered" and are re-living the pain from the original hurt.[21]

It is no wonder that the pain feels intense, but if we incorrectly think we are reacting to the current situation, rather than recognizing the feelings are based on an earlier situation, then we will misdiagnose how we need to address it. Dr. Curt

Note on Brain Science

It is also in this region of the brain that scientists have discovered where affection for transcendence resides. Transcendence enriches our identity when we realize that we are connected not only to the temporal and physical, but also to God.

A new study published in *Cerebral Cortex* suggests that when part of our left hemisphere calms, we are significantly more open to experience the transcendent. This study suggests that the connection takes place in the Parietal Lobe behind the Prefrontal Cortex (PFC). If the suggestions of the study are correct, isn't it amazing that our experience of God is next to the place in the brain where our True Identity resides!

[1] Miller L, Balodis IM, McClintock CH, et al. (2019) Neural correlates of personalized spiritual experiences. Cerebral Cortex (29) 6: 2331–2338.

---

[21] Siegel, *The Developing Mind, op. cit.*, p. 52.

Thompson calls this process "the low road."[22]

> *For example, when I was very young – about 4 years old – my mother decided to go shopping. I wanted to go along, but she said, "You are not ready," and went out the door. Although she never would have left me home alone with no one else there, in my memory, I am standing at the door crying and feeling completely abandoned and alone. (This is an example of "attachment pain," in which we feel grief or pain because an attachment that we think should have taken place did not happen).*
>
> *After that experience, any time I heard the words, "You are not ready," or was in a situation in which I felt like I was being left out, I experienced a stab of sadness and abandonment. It was only when I learned to invite Jesus into the painful situation that He was able to show me that I was not alone (He is always with us!).*
>
> *When I invited Jesus back into that early abandonment pain, I asked Him to show me where He was and what He wanted to say to me. When He showed me that He had been there and was reaching out to me, I was able to reinterpret the situation and to realize that I was neither hopeless nor alone. That early wound was healed, and I could proceed in life with a new awareness of His presence.*

---

[22] Thompson, Curt. (2010) *Anatomy of the Soul*. Tyndale Momentum, p. 165.

Chapter 7
Level Five-Our Library Function in the Left Hemisphere

Some authors on brain science refer to the left hemisphere of the brain as Level Five. Andrew Miller calls this "Function."[23] It is the part of the brain with which we have the most familiarity because we can directly access it. It is the place where we make decisions, catalog experiences, and name things.

Discovering Our True Identity

With all the possibilities for getting our internal identity "compass" out of whack, what hope is there for us? Our true identity is found in Christ. We should turn to Him to hear what He has to say about who we are. HeartSync's Andrew Miller calls this our "Original Self."[24]

So how do we discover our true identity? We can begin by expressing appreciation for at least five minutes, recalling various things for which we are grateful, including the relational appreciation we share with others such as a beautiful sunset enjoyed with someone else. It could also be celebrating something with the Lord. Having a great meal with friends. Beautiful music. Art. Family. The more we express appreciation for those things, and the greater detail we can muster, the more our relational circuits turn on. Dr. Karl Lehman describes it as being similar to putting your foot on the gas pedal. The car begins to accelerate, but it does not reach its maximum speed immediately. It keeps accelerating. So, too, with appreciation: our brain engages increasing joy the more we express appreciation, growing our experience and ultimately growing our capacity for joy.[25]

The attunement that can occur is not only with a person or people around us; it can also take place with the mind of Christ. It is one of the most amazing and wonderful things in human life, that the Creator wants to link with us, His creation, in a personal and intimate way. He can reveal His thoughts to us and has ways of transforming our lives, simply by giving us input about His presence.

---

[23] Miller, Andrew, *HeartSync, op. cit.*
[24] Miller, Andrew, *HeartSync, op. cit.*
[25] Lehman, Karl. "Positive Memory Prayer" February 5, 2018. Brown Line Vineyard Podcasts.

If we would like to get Jesus' take on a negative experience when we felt alone or experienced some other fear, after expressing appreciation and attuning with the mind of Christ, we should remember that although we *felt* alone, we actually *were never alone*. Jesus is Immanuel, which literally means "God with us." He is there with us in celebration, and He is there with us when we are in pain, even if we don't realize it. We should ask Him two questions:

1, Where are you Lord in this memory?
2. What do you want to say to me?

The truths that Jesus expresses to us are the very best way for us to come to an understanding of what our identity truly is.

Having spoken with many people who have done this, it takes my breath away to hear what the Lord says to them. Many people expect Jesus, as the thoroughly holy God, to speak judgment or condemnation, but He doesn't.

> *One person said that they heard him say, "I am tender to your weakness." What an amazing statement. It doesn't ignore sin, weakness, or failure, but neither does it condemn. It is actually a friendly encouragement to "come up higher," and choose to walk in more holiness. It is hard to imagine how anyone else could be as affirming, convicting, loving, accepting, and encouraging all at the same time! But that is precisely Who Jesus is!*

> *Another person, a woman in her early thirties, shared how her life had always been characterized by pain of failure. When she was five years old, she had been left at home alone with her two-year-old brother, being told she was responsible for baby-sitting him. Somehow a fire broke out. She managed to rescue her brother, but the house burned to the ground. Her self-image was of being irresponsible and being a failure. In prayer, Jesus spoke to her and answered the question, "Where are you, Lord." As He revealed His presence to her, it was at the scene of the fire as she stood in the front yard watching her home burn down. She felt terrible responsibility, thought her pain was misplaced. Obviously, her parents should never have left a five-year old babysitting and in charge!*

> *When the Lord showed her the truth, she gasped, "The Fireman! Jesus was the Fireman!" A kindhearted fire-fighter had given teddy bears to her and her brother and said, "It is not your fault.*

You have not failed. You succeeded. You saved your brother. You are a hero!" He had said that thirty-three years before, but she was not able to hear and assimilate it. Now, in prayer, it sunk into her heart and life. In a matter of seconds, the Lord had transformed her self-image from being an irresponsible failure to seeing herself rightly as a heroic little girl who had rescued her brother from not only the dangerous situation of being left alone with her at home, but she had also rescued him from the fire! She was heroic indeed, and the Lord convinced her of it in a matter of seconds of revelation.

The Brain Throughout the Body

As we said earlier, many people think of the brain as being solely "cranial," or contained in the cranium, or head. In fact, it is "somatic." *Soma* is the Greek/medical word for body. The brain actually extends throughout the body because the nervous system is not located only inside the head; rather, nerves permeate the entire body from fingertips and toes to the top of the head.

Amazingly, Dr. Siegel points out that it does not actually stop with our body.[26] He shares a story of his brain so powerfully syncing with a patient that his body began reacting like hers, from tapping of his foot like her, to his heart accelerating to match her anxiety. Because we have numerous mechanisms for interface (e.g., touch, hearing, smell, taste, and eye contact), a linking can take place from one person to another like a brain-to-brain direct WI-FI of sorts. In other words, when two people have their "relational circuits" on and "attachment lights" on, this syncing takes place.

The term *relational circuits* refers to the openness to connect with other people in a significant way. When one's relational circuits are on, they have a sensitivity to other people around them. They have a willingness to connect and care for the other person, and a desire for relational prosperity. The cingulate cortex is a treasure chest of relationship tools and celebration when it is working correctly. When we have not developed the skills to attune with others, and this level is not properly fulfilling its purpose, we can get stuck and enter into lackluster, superficial, or even pathological relationships.[27]

---

[26] Siegel, *Developing Mind, op. cit.*, p. 93.
[27] Warner and Wilder, *Rare Leadership, op. cit.*, p. 69.

A woman I know, (let's call her "Alice"), is very bright and hard driving. She is task-oriented and is extremely productive, but the fallout is tremendous. Watching her work and interact with other people, one can easily see her productivity, but there is a wake of devastated relationships that follows her. She gets things done, but it is often at the expense of relationships. Whatever the actual condition of her heart, many people get the idea that they don't matter to her, and walk away rather than engage in a relationship in which they feel "steamrolled."

I am looking for the opportunity to share about relational circuits with her. If she does not get some understanding, she is going to become increasingly isolated. Many of us know people like Alice who are very productive in accomplishing tasks, but very destructive in terms of relationships.

Remember, when our attachment lights are on and our relational circuits are on, we are in a "mutual mind" state, we are syncing with another person, and we are able to "build joy." In my experience, attunement quickly bears fruit. When my wife Susan and I began regularly pursuing joy smiles and attunement, I did not expect much to happen. What actually happened, though, was that I was shocked to feel our relationship changing very quickly as we invested in attuning. In the first few weeks, I could tell there was a new depth and much greater joy. Over the last several years, I would have to use a term like "revolutionary" to describe how powerfully our marriage has been enriched, simply by pursuing joy smiles and attunement. Susan sees similar fruit, and she will often say, "How about some joy smiles and attuning?" throughout the day.

As we go on, I'll describe ways the Lord (and my Grandfather!) have led me to recover from negative emotions and recapture the joy the Lord wants us to experience. Your pathway to recapture joy will have its own characteristics but will share some elements with my story. One of the key factors is the role that another person plays in helping us return to joy. While that person can be Jesus, certainly when we are starting to return to joy, it will likely be with another person. Eventually, we can learn to rely on Him to help us quiet and return to the joy in which we were designed to live.

Chapter 8
Joy
What It Is and What It Isn't

When I was a boy, my growing up years were spent in Germany, where my father was a military officer. He was a Battalion Commander of the 82nd Infantry, as the U.S. Army of Occupation was in Germany after World War II. It is hard to believe that we went to Germany as a family less than ten years after the war ended. I remember that there were still bombed out factories and structures everywhere, as well as countless buildings with pock marks from bullets. When we first moved there, I was only about six years old, so I didn't have much of a world view beyond the four walls of our home. That perspective was greatly expanded as we were plopped down in a different country, culture, and language. Somehow, I processed it as a wonderful great adventure, probably because my Grandfather had instilled in me an appreciation for sharing when he once said to me, "I hope you will discover what I have learned, that real joy, real satisfaction comes from sharing what you have far more than acquiring something for yourself."

> *From the General:*
> I hope you will discover what I have learned, that real joy, real satisfaction comes from sharing what you have far more than acquiring something for yourself.
> -- Brig. Gen. James A. Pickering

I can't blame my father for being absent for almost all of the first five years of my life. He was off fighting in the Korean War. God's wisdom and vision connected me with my grandfather during all those years. My Grandfather became a stable presence and secure attachment provider for me.

Fiend or Friend?

Almost anyone will tell you that if you visit another culture, the one thing you absolutely must not do is attempt humor. You will soon learn that cross-cultural attempts at humor absolutely will not work. Even at my tender age, I was well aware of that axiom, but I completely disregarded it! One of the big factors leading me to ignore the advice was Herr Schmitt. Herr Schmitt was *der Feuerwehrmann* [the fireman]. Every morning, he would come early, just as daylight was beginning (or for that matter, even before), and shovel coal from a big bin on the side of the house into a chute that fed coal into the furnace for the house.

I used to love hanging with him. I wasn't able to shovel coal, but I would stand there listening to him tell stories. At first, I couldn't understand any of it, but as time went on, my every-morning ritual with Herr Schmitt yielded more and more understanding of the German language, and a window into German culture and humor.

> *For example, every morning, as he was first arriving, I would greet him with the colloquial greeting, "Was is lose?" Meaning "what's up?" but literally meaning "What is loose?" With belly laughing glee, every day his reply was the same and would play on the literal meaning of the words in my question rather than on the normal colloquial meaning.*
>
> *So to my "Was is lose?" [Pronounced Vas ess lowse?] Herr Schmitt would reply: Die hund is lose [The dog is loose.] and be convulsed with laughter. Every day, it was the same thing: my question and his wacky play-on-words answer.*
>
> *It was not a common response. In fact, in the years we lived in Germany, I never heard anyone else use that play-on-words. It was a special bonding joy between an elderly man (who was overjoyed to have a job of any kind after the brutalities of war) and a little boy who was new to the country and culture. After our greeting and mutual laughter, we would talk. At first, our conversations were very halting due to my very limited vocabulary, so there was a lot of non-verbal gesturing, but I have since learned that non-verbal communication helps brains attune. It didn't take long for my German language skills to develop. Herr Schmitt's German instruction was far more effective than were the German language classes I had every day in school. Even now, many years later, Germans will still take my accent as native and are surprised to learn that I am not a German.*
>
> *I didn't see Herr Schmitt as a vanquished enemy. He was my friend. One of my first real ones. I didn't see his circumstances as humiliating—he had too much joy to see them that way himself, and as a result, neither did I. In retrospect, it was not much of a job for a man to have, especially in his later years, but it did not matter to the community we experienced. With just*

my un-anxious and unjudging presence, I ministered to him in the pain of his post-war life, and he to me – stranger, alien, and boy in need of connection.

After half a year or more of the same question, his same answer, and our mutual laughter, it would be silly to maintain that the laughter and the joy were actually a response to the humor of the situation. Instead, the joy was a result of relationship – relating and connecting, linking, and laughing. The level of joy was not from something funny; it was from something mutual and profound. It was a mutual treasure, the gladness of being together and sharing life in the simplest of tasks – shoveling coal. It was not merely the coal; it was the twinkle of his eye and the knowledge that he was glad to be with me. For my part, I enjoyed our every-morning ritual before school at a profound level. It gave me a sense of belonging. It gave me roots, and it expanded my understanding of who my people were. It was not just my natural family from America; it was also these people who had been just a few years previously an enemy to be vanquished. Now, after the military victory, the task was rebuilding, and Herr Schmitt and I embraced our calling deeply, and we did so well.

This kind of joy is what we were designed to have—connection with another person (or people) in everyday life. The origins of this kind of joy are absolutely ancient—from God's first creative acts in heaven. He designed His creatures, both angelic and human, to resonate together in joy. The proper order of creation was for us to abide in that joy. The terrible consequences of the Fall have distorted and robbed it from us, but thanks to the redemptive work of Jesus on the Cross and His Resurrection, we can be healed and will forever live in joy again. Happily, we can learn to live more in joy than we have been doing. When sinful circumstances steal our joy, we can learn how to recapture it.

Joy vs. Pleasure

Jim Wilder makes the profound observation that joy is not pleasure. Pleasure can be experienced in the lowest levels of our brain, well beneath the cognitive layer, where it is just sensation and not relationship. In order to experience joy, we must have relationship. The best is when we have a circle of relationships of substance, so we have community.

Joy occurs when our brain is attuned (or synced) with the brain of another person, and we share life — not merely things that we celebrate, but the place where we expose our weaknesses and are loved despite them. It is that place where the strong and the weak live together in a way that makes both of them more than they would be without the other.[28]

One may well ask, "Why were these conversations with a man shoveling coal so significant?" There may well be other reasons, but I can think of two. The first is the amount of time that was invested in our meetings. I saw Herr Schmitt every day. It wasn't for a long time…maybe 15 or 20 minutes each day, but it was intentional, and over time, the amount of cumulative time really added up to a lot of hours. Attachment requires time. The flip side is that when we spend a lot of time with something or someone, attachments will form. Attachment is a key factor to being able to form secure bonds that are the platform for relational richness.

Warm, kind, and redemptive fellowship expresses the Father's love. No wonder it can bear great fruit. It is this kind of joyful fellowship for which we are made. Our "hearts" crave it.

The second reason that the times with my coal-shoveling friend were important is that they provided a predictable, regular, warm kind of fellowship. That kind of relationship mirrors (in a small way) the fellowship in heaven among God the Father, God the Son, and God the Holy Spirit. When we do some of what He does, it tends to welcome His manifest presence (also called the *Fruit of the Spirit*) into our lives. (Conversely, when people ardently pursue sin, doing so tends to welcome the manifest presence of demonic pests!).

Warm, kind, and redemptive fellowship expresses the Father's love. No wonder it can bear great fruit. It is this kind of joyful fellowship for which we are made. Our "hearts" crave it.

Actually, though, our heart is just a muscle that pumps blood. What is really doing the craving is not the heart; it is the right hemisphere of our brain — that's what the Bible means when it talks about the human heart, the formerly hidden repository of memories and relationships. It is a processing powerhouse that builds identity that (at least subconsciously) articulates who we are and sets a course for how we are going to act. It is what we really want and what we really need; and it is powerfully at

---

[28] Wilder, *Joy Starts Here, op. cit.,* pg. 5.

work even when we don't realize it is doing it. Now with research that MRIs have made possible, we are discovering how to harvest relational treasure.

When Jesus says, "These things I have spoken to you, that My joy may remain in you, and [that] your joy may be full," He is not saying that irritation and disappointment will be taken away. Nor is He offering some superficial or passing pleasure. He is saying that He will fill us to the point that what we have in Him and in His people gives us joy even when we hurt. It is important to understand that joy is not the absence of trials. It is the fullness of heart that people have when they are loved and known as they truly are. It is the fullness of heart that we have when we know we have been used of the Lord to minister to another person. It is the feeling that is evoked in the stanza of a current song that says, "I will hold your people in my heart." Many people never know that kind of love. Once tasted, though, the desire is deep to return to return to it:

"As the deer pants for the water brooks,
So pants my soul for You, O God"
(Psalm 421).

Chapter 9
Recapturing Joy from DESPAIR

I lack the time and resources for this! ... And I can't change it!
...but God has the resources I need and don't have.

The loss of control over events, situations, or people in our lives is one of the most destabilizing and fearful feelings we can experience. When we are despondent but know that we can recover from something, what we feel is unpleasant but not overwhelming. When circumstances have rolled over us like a tidal wave, and we know we have no control, we are devastated – and that's when despair occurs. On our own, we are not going to experience freedom, security, or joy. We need to connect with others who bring additional resources and encouragement.

When I was a boy, I used to fiddle with radios. One of the strongest stations in North America was just across the border from Del Rio, Texas, in Ciudad Acuna, Coahuila. It's call sign was XERF. It was audible even with a simple homemade crystal radio set because at one million watts (!), it was many times more powerful than most U.S. stations. The U.S. allowed a maximum of only 50,000 watts. Most of the night was spent on XERF with shouting radio evangelists denouncing sin. I still remember an American radio preacher who had bought time on the Mexican station shouting, "Because of your sin, you are a stench in the nostrils of God." Except, he drew out God to be several syllables, something like, "Gawwww-wadd," and he repeated himself over and over.

> *In my life, that redemptive love has had many faces, but one of the most important ones was the despair that led to encountering Jesus Christ as living hope.*

I knew two things. First of all, even though I grieved my own sin well enough, I didn't feel like a nostril stench. Secondly, I knew that the angry radio guy didn't have anything I wanted. But that doesn't mean that I didn't need *anything!* I desperately needed to come into a relationship with Jesus and let Him take His rightful place in my life.

God's creative momentum is so powerful that He not only creates when things are new, He re-creates and redeems when things are terrible. In my life, that redemptive love has had many faces, but one of the most important ones was the despair that led to encountering Jesus Christ as living hope.

When I was a young Air Force pilot, people regularly told me how much they envied my life. I was flying all over the world, had a job with challenge and responsibility, and was being paid more money than I could spend (though not more than I could waste!).

Something, however, was amiss. There was a deep disquiet inside me. I knew that there was something missing, but I didn't know what it was.

Waking up one morning, just lying in bed and looking up at the ceiling, I noticed a cobweb in the corner of the ceiling. As I lay there thinking, my heart was aching. It was like there was a great weight on me. What was so utterly distressing was the awareness that I had actually accomplished the goals I had set, and yet, I realized that I was not even a single step closer to finding fulfillment. It felt like there was a hole in my heart.

From the General:
When I lost my eye, at first, I was in despair. I thought I had lost everything, but I realized I needed to surrender to the situation and wait. I expected to be told to pursue a different career, but the answer came by way of a special piece of legislation in Congress authorizing me to serve with one eye. In adverse circumstances, we need to see what plan develops. Something always will.

-- Brig. Gen. James A. Pickering

I just lay there in bed thinking, with despair rising. Teardrop pools were filling my eyes — but didn't roll off because I was still on my back in bed. It was a deeper pain than I had ever experienced: not like a broken toe or skinned knee, but painful, nonetheless. What was especially bad was the awareness that I did not have any idea what to do to fix it. Solutions had always come pretty easily. Goals were usually readily met, but now I found myself in a situation about which I had no idea what to do — how to fill the gaping emptiness.

Out of the blue, I remembered a strange conversation I had had in pilot training. I had gone out on the perimeter road around the Air Force base late at night to look at the amazing number of stars. We were out in the desert and away from city lights. The sky was remarkable. Awestruck, I was just leaning back on my car looking up and did not notice the guy who came up to me until he spoke.

"In every man, there is a God-shaped void that only Jesus Christ can fill. Remember that. It is going to be important in your life."

I didn't know him. I hadn't met him before and didn't think much of what he said at the time, but now it was reverberating in my thinking.

Could that be it? Could it be as simple as turning my life over to Jesus? But, all the people I know who have done that are weird. Do I want to be weird?

Then another thought broke in. It was like someone was feeding thoughts to me.

Does it matter if I become weird if I am fulfilled and happy?

I got up from bed. As I sat up, the teardrop pools that had been in my eyes rolled down my cheeks. My day started while pondering. *Is this true? A God-shaped void?* There was certainly deep despair from the knowledge that I didn't have the resources to fix this situation, but there was a spark of something—hope—that there might be an answer. I wondered if Jesus might be that answer.

The phone rang. Cindy, the wife of another pilot was on the phone. Her husband and I had been in pilot training together but were not close at all. We just didn't click.

She said, "I had to call to tell you what happened to me. When my husband went on a long overseas trip, I went home to Indiana to spend some time with family. While I was there, I was invited to a ladies' coffee. We drank coffee for a while, then all of a sudden, they all put down their coffee cups and began to pray. I'd never heard anything like it. They were all talking to Jesus, but differently than any prayers I had heard before. They talked to Him like he was *actually* there—like he was listening and cared!"

She continued, "I was leaning back on the sofa listening and thinking. I realized I had never considered the possibility that Jesus might actually be alive; that He might be listening. I said, 'Jesus, if You are real, I would serve You!'

"Suddenly, I don't know how, I knew it was true. He was revealing Himself to me. He is real. He's alive. I've never felt such love. I knew I had to tell you. Actually, you are so obnoxious I know you must be looking for something!"

Despite the slam, I had to laugh. Not only was she right that something was missing, and I was looking to fill it, Jesus was obviously orchestrating things to reach out to me. It was enough to push me toward making a commitment to Jesus as Lord. She and her husband invited me to meet them at a church they had found nearby. It was the evening of Easter Sunday. I don't remember the message, or the people. I remember the music, that it was very lively, and they had a trombone. What I recall most vividly is the clarity of the choice that was before me. As I sat thinking, it was clear to me that I wanted to respond to the Lord's pursuit and make a commitment in return.

I prayed, "Lord Jesus, I will go wherever You say, 'Go.' Lord Jesus, I will do whatever You say I should do. Lord Jesus, I will be wherever You say to be, and I will say whatever you tell me to say. I only ask two things: Be real in my life and satisfy this emptiness inside me."

At that moment something happened; it was not particularly an emotional experience, but it was a real one. Somehow, I knew it was true. I knew He was there, and I knew I was forever different. It was utterly amazing. The externals of my life had not changed, but my life was revolutionized.

What moves people to make a commitment to Christ is a sense of deep need, even desperation, that there is something amiss in their lives that they are not able to remedy.

The heart of despair is to realize that we do not have the resources that we need, and we do not even have a way to acquire them. For years, the evangelical world has offered a series of Gospel presentations that intended to bring people into a relationship with Jesus. Virtually all of them are based on delivering people from sin. The problem is that sin is not the agenda of the seeker, but despair is.

For several years when traveling around the country, I would ask, "For those who have a personal relationship with Jesus Christ, how many of you would say that it was the burden of your sins that moved you to make a commitment to Christ?"

In almost five years of asking that question, the only people sho raised their hands to answer "yes," were convicted felons in a prison I visited! Pretty much everyone else shared how an unmet need in their life was what led to faith in Jesus Christ.

My next question was, "For those of you who would say that you have come to faith in Jesus Christ, have you come to a place being deeply moved to admit your own sins and sinfulness?" Virtually every hand would go up.

What moves people to make a commitment to Christ is a sense of deep need, even desperation, that there is something in their life that they are not able to address. Often, when we are talking with someone and they express a deep need, those of us who have been trained in one of the classic Gospel presentations may try to turn the conversation from their need, to talking about sin.

For example, if someone says, "My teen is on drugs." Or "I have cancer," "My roof leaks," "I had a bad medical diagnosis," or "I'm afraid I'm going to lose my job," we have basically been trained to say, "Well that aside, your real problem is that you are a sinner, separated from Jesus Christ because of your sin. Put that other problem on the back burner, and let's deal with your bigger problem: your sin."

At this point, they are not motivated to listen. It is one of the reasons why our conversion rates are low!

If, however, when someone says, "I have cancer," we reply, "Oh, my goodness, I'm so sorry. I do want to tell you that not only do I care about that, but Jesus does as well. If we ask Him, He promises that He will be with you. I can't tell you *how* He will help, but I believe His promise that He will!"

This leads me to a simple pattern of sharing Jesus, especially for those in despair who do not have the resources that they need for life. Usually, when someone is moving toward making a commitment to Jesus Christ, there is a person who has exhibited the kindness of Jesus. It is usually a relationship like that which motivates people toward taking the next step spiritually. Perhaps you have a need like that in your life. I'll bet you can identify someone who has demonstrated the kindness of Jesus to you. If you would like to take a step in your spiritual life, or you are talking with someone who longs to have a change in their life, here is a simple pattern you can follow: A, B, C, D.

A. Something to *Admit*

Admit that there is a need in your life that is beyond your control. It may be a need for love, forgiveness, or healing. Or it may just be the need to have a void in your life filled.

B. Something to *Believe*

Make the decision to trust that Jesus is the One He claims to be and that He can be trusted to help your need.

C. Something to *Confess*

Make your relationship with Jesus personal with the positive confession that "Jesus Christ is Lord."

D. Something to *Do*

Commit to follow Jesus in the fellowship of His church and order your life according to His Principles.

The wonderful truth is that Jesus is the one Who pursues us. We do not have to convince Him to enter into a relationship with us. He literally died so we could have one! Any outreach that we make will be met with more kindness than we can imagine. It is His greatest desire that we find peace in the midst of life's storms and that we get started on a pathway of relationship and eternal life. That relationship with Him will be key in returning to joy when hopeless despair strikes again!

In times of returning to joy from hopeless despair, you can find your own pathway, but it could well be similar to this:

- Make sure relational circuits are on.
- Tap into a supportive connection with another person (human or Jesus).
- Take five minutes or more to express appreciation with someone.
- Invite Jesus to show you where He is in the midst of your despair.
- Listen to the voice of the Lord (or the other person).
- Invite the Lord to speak.
- Listen for insight into the situation.
- Obey the leading He is offering.

The heart of despair is the overwhelming sense that "I lack the time and resources for this! ...And, I can't change it!" For me, at the heart of recapturing joy in despair is the way that Jesus reinterprets everything by His presence.

In the midst of despair, when I focus on Him, He reassures me and gives me peace. Certainly a knowledge of Scripture is helpful as He highlights or reminds me of promises that are found in the Bible.

One of the first and primal fears in despair is that I lack the capacity to protect myself. To that, Scripture speaks powerfully that He is my "strong tower" and defense!

To the leader: with stringed instruments. Of David.

> *Hear my cry, O God;*
> *listen to my prayer.*
> *From the end of the earth I call to you,*
> *when my heart is faint.*
> *Lead me to the rock*
> *that is higher than I;*
> *for you are my refuge,*
> *a strong tower against the enemy. (Psalm 61:1-3)*

He also promises to supply what I need.

> *And my God will fully satisfy every need of yours according to his riches in glory in Christ Jesus (Philippians 4:19)*

The heart of despair is the sense that I do not have the resources necessary to meet the needs in the current crisis. In fact, that is believing a lie. We are not meant to have all the resources necessary. Our contribution is significant, but minor. We are like the small boy at the feeding of the 5,000 who had five loaves and two fish. That was not enough to feed the crowd, unless you do your calculations by heavenly kingdom math, whereby God multiplies what little we have to offer. When I remember that truth, He reassures me that I am safe and that He has the resources for the crisis at hand, which helps me recapture joy, even in the midst of despair.

Chapter 10
Recapturing Joy from SADNESS

*Sadness comes when our expectations are not met,
and I feel like <u>I have lost something</u> of my life.*

The Fourth of July in Texas can have temperatures so severe they could make a frying pan blush. We usually gather the family during the day and alternate between the air conditioning inside and meat on the grill out back. We generally hang around all day until our neighborhood fireworks display at dusk. The fireworks are always spectacular, and we look forward to them—especially my grandchildren.

In the middle of the morning on a recent Fourth of July, my 10-year-old granddaughter was complaining that she really felt terrible. She had a fever, and it was increasing. Over the course of a couple hours, she got increasingly worse. Finally, her mother and I took her to Children's Hospital. It is famous for amazing, high quality care, but we didn't know what to expect because it was a holiday.

The doctors were excellent and compassionate, but they could not be definitive. They said it was presenting like appendicitis, but her abdomen was not sensitive to touch. They said that they needed to do an x-ray—maybe a sonogram—to find out what was going on.

It took only a few minutes to organize the imaging, but she was getting worse. They got the images and determined that it was, in fact, appendicitis, and they were almost sure that the appendix had already ruptured.

"The problem," the ER doctor explained, "is that she has what is called a 'retrograde appendix.' That means that instead of hanging down like most people's, her appendix goes back horizontally and is wedged in tightly. That is why she was able to withstand it rupturing without collapsing in pain. The pressure kept the pain down. The problem now, however, is that since it has ruptured, the infection is all over the place. Basically, she is too sick to operate. We have to try to get her better before we can operate. Right now, she is just too sick."

While it was helpful to get more information, the fact that she was too sick to undergo surgery was extremely alarming.

Then the doctor looked like he had an idea. "Who's on call for surgery today?"

The nurse immediately replied with the name of the head of pediatric surgery. "He always takes call on holidays so other doctors can have time with their families."

"Who's on for anesthesiology?"

The nurse replied, "The department head."

Then the doctor turned to us and said, "You really must lead blessed lives! I had said that we couldn't operate. Normally that's true, but this combination of surgeon and anesthesiologist may be the best pair in the world. I don't know anyone else that could do this surgery, but I think they probably can. I'm going to call him now and see."

We immediately began to pray. He must have been close by, because in only about fifteen minutes the surgeon came through the door of the treatment room.

He introduced himself and said, "I've looked at the images and talked with the anesthesiologist. He's on his way in. Right now we are going to prep her for surgery and get started as soon as he arrives. You have a sick little girl, but we are going to do our best to make sure she gets better."

Both her mother (my daughter) and I were relieved. We called the rest of the family. Grammy took the watch duty for the other grandchildren from their dad so he could join us at the hospital.

By the time her Dad arrived, they were ready to wheel my granddaughter into surgery. We prayed, and I anointed her and sent her off with earnest prayers surrounding her.

Some hours later, the surgeon came out to brief us. "We had a successful surgery. She is going to be OK, but there will be a rough time of recovery. The infection had spread internally across her abdominal organs. Everything is raw from the infection. We cleaned out what we could, but there will have to be follow-up treatments to keep irrigating it and washing out the infection."

Eventually, we got her out of recovery and settled into a room. While we were all relieved, the treatment that they were going to use for follow-up was *horrible*. A port had been installed into her abdomen. Saline (salt water) had to be pumped into her abdominal cavity and then drained out to irrigate all the infected organs. The problem was like the old proverb about rubbing salt into a wound, and that is *exactly* what they were going to do! To add to the problem, there was nothing that could be done to alleviate the pain while doing it. They were concerned that any pain medications would depress her respiration too much.

I'm sure it was terrible news for her mother, but it was also incredibly sad for me. The thought of my sweet ten-year-old granddaughter having to suffer was heartbreaking. That was only exacerbated when they started the treatments. They were horrible torture. I couldn't even imagine the pain for my sweet granddaughter. It was one of the saddest times in my life.

> From the General:
> When you have to face something negative you can face something painful today, or face something more painful tomorrow.
> -- Brig. Gen. James A. Pickering

My grandfather's advice was some comfort. When asked about how to deal with something negative, he told me that, "When you have to face something negative, you can face something painful today…or face something more painful tomorrow." That was certainly the case in this instance. My precious granddaughter would have to face so much pain in the present, but it was to spare her more pain in the future, and actually, it was saving her life.

I retreated to a quiet place and was praying urgently for the Lord to intervene. I prayed to ask him what to do. The strong sensation came to me to hold her during the treatment and pray quietly into her ear in the Spirit. It is also called praying in tongues, a heavenly language shaped by the Holy Spirit to be the perfect prayer. To the speaker and the listener, it just sounds like a foreign language that you don't know or understand, but in the Spiritual realm, the Bible says it edifies and builds us up. I knew I had to reach out and care for her.

> *When they finished, she said, "Grandpa, this time when you prayed in tongues it hardly hurt at all. I loved the sound of it. It's late tonight. Tomorrow can we pray for me to get a prayer language?"*

When she had the treatment this time, I held her tightly in my arms and prayed. She didn't cry out. When they finished, she said, "Grandpa, this time when you prayed in tongues it hardly hurt at all. I loved the sound of it. It's late tonight. Tomorrow can we pray for me to get a prayer language?"

Age 10. Not sad anymore. Me either!

The next day, I visited with her about the power of the Spirit. She had been a believer for years already. I told her:

"Remember hearing about Colorado where I took your mother on a snowmobile? We went to the Continental Divide."

"Yes," she said. "That's the place where a raindrop on one side would flow through streams and rivers into the Pacific and on the other side, would go to the Gulf of Mexico and the Atlantic."

"That's right. Well, there is another 'Continental Divide' as well. It has to do with whether or not people are in Christ, or not in Christ. If they are believers in Jesus, they are in Christ. If they are not believers then they are not in Christ. Of those who are in Christ, there is another distinction. Some people say, 'Lord I will follow you and I will live my life to the fullness of all the strength I have.' Others say, 'Lord I will follow you and live my life with all of the strength I have, but I also invite you to work in me and through me supernaturally.' Do you see how that is different?"

"Sure," she said, and added (with wisdom far beyond her years), "I can serve Jesus with all my heart, but I don't have any miracles inside me. He would have to do that. But, Grandpa, I want the miracle stuff!"

"OK, honey. You can get Holy Spirit power! Here's how:

- First, you should pray to recommit your life to Jesus. I always ask people to do that because it is important that we insure they are believers before praying for supernatural power.
- Second, pray in your own words asking the Lord for the power of the Holy Spirit. Let Him know that you want Him to work in you and through you supernaturally.
- Third, you don't have to, but you can ask Him for a spiritual prayer language.
- Fourth, just begin to pray and praise Him, but don't do it in English, just whatever syllables and sounds come out.

I went on to tell her a story

> *"One of my favorite stories was from some friends at a church in New Jersey. It was a Pentecostal Church, so they put a huge emphasis on praying in tongues. There was a guy who would go to the front of the church after every service, Sunday morning,*

Sunday evening, and Wednesday night. He would cry out, 'Lord, I want to pray in tongues...Give me tongues!' and would do that every service.

The people were getting really tired of him crying out and asking. Then a visiting preacher said, "Remember, 'they spoke with other tongues as the Spirit gave utterance.' Utterance is the place in your brain where thoughts are turned to words you speak or sounds you hear are turned into thoughts. When you pray in the Spirit, though, the speech center is bypassed and the Holy Spirit is shaping what is said. It can feel random or even like you are making up sounds."

Then the man who had been praying to pray in tongues for years actually began to speak. This went on for several minutes, much to the relief of the people who had grown tired of his very vocal asking! After a few minutes, he stopped and said, 'Wait, that wasn't real. I was just making it up!!'

Two young Asian men were visiting the church and were seated in the second row. They said, "Very interesting that you were making that up, it was in our original home dialect and you were speaking about the love and greatness of God!"

It didn't matter how he felt. Once he had prayed and then began speaking, the Holy Spirit was shaping his words."

"OK, Grandpa. I get it. Let's pray!"

She began to pray, "Lord Jesus, thank you for the beautiful world you have given to us. Thank you for sharing it with us and letting us get to know You. I recommit my life to you."

Imagine the joy I experienced to hear her pray like that when she had been in the hospital for almost three weeks, much of the time in terrible pain. Despite that, she saw the world as beautiful and the Lord as only good.

I had tears in my eyes as she prayed. Then as she finished that prayer, she began praying in the Spirit, like a little motor running! As she prayed, her eyes popped open and she had an amazing smile on her face.

Then she turned to look at me and said, "The devil tried to kill me with this nasty appendix attack, but God knew better. He gave me great doctors. Jesus filled me with the Holy Spirit and gave me tongues. How great is that!"

Yes, my child. How great is that! Sadness dispelled. Joy recaptured!

In recapturing joy from sadness, here is what I have discovered:

- Make sure relational circuits are on.
- Turn to Jesus for quieting.
- Tap into a supportive connection with another person (human or Jesus).
- Recall Scriptural promises in which you can hear the voice of the Lord (or the other person) showing you how to change your perspective.
- Watch for ways that the Lord (or a bonded friend) says to you that He is enough.
- Celebrate what you have and who you are in Christ. Do not let the lack define you.

Sadness grips me when I have the realization that I have lost something of my life. In this case, it was the loss of peace and joy in my granddaughter's life. In the midst of the great sadness, there was also the deep sadness I experienced realizing that we could lose her. Knowing what I needed, the Lord pointed me to the experience of King David of Israel, who said

> *You have turned my mourning into dancing;*
> *You have taken of my sackcloth and clothed me with joy,*
> *So that my soul may praise you and not be silent.*
> *O LORD my God, I will give thanks to you forever. (Psalm 30:11-12)*

When I think things are too far gone and what is lost is gone forever, Jesus often reminds me:

> *I will restore to you the years*
> *that the swarming locust has eaten,*
> *the hopper, the destroyer, and the cutter,*
> *my great army, which I sent against you.*
> *You shall eat in plenty and be satisfied*
> *And praise the name of the LORD your God,*
> *Who has dealt wondrously with you. (Joel 2:25-26)*

It is not just that Jesus is able to restore conceptually. He is actually the restorer in fact!

Chapter 11

Recapturing Joy from ANGER

I need to protect myself and <u>make it stop</u>.

When we are assaulted by circumstances that overwhelm us, our natural response is to want to protect ourselves. We want the pain and unpleasantness to stop, stop, stop! A knee-jerk response is to strike out, usually at a person or people around us. Tragically, the persons we wound may not have anything to do with what caused the anger. They are just the convenient target of our anger and frustration. The subconscious process is that striking out against *something* will make us feel better, but it is actually learning to quiet ourselves and recapture our joy that is the solution.

My story about recapturing joy from anger takes a longer description to set the stage for why and just how seriously angry I was.

The German telephone rang in short, staccato bursts in my hotel room, and I reached for it in the dark. I found my watch but couldn't see the time.

"Captain Atwood? This is the Duty Officer at the ACP (Airlift Command Post). Please pack your bag immediately. There will be someone to meet you downstairs in ten minutes. I can't tell you any more over the phone."

"I'm sorry," groggily I protested, "There must be some mistake. We just got into Frankfurt a couple of hours ago; it must be three o'clock here, and I don't even know what time it really is; my stomach's still somewhere in New Jersey."

He didn't seem to appreciate my protest. "The man from the State Department will fill you in. The rest of your crew will continue the mission that you were on. You have ten minutes."

The whole exchange hardly took a minute and hadn't awakened my roommate.

I shook him, "Dave, Command Post just called -- they said someone from the State Department was going to take me to another hotel to join up with another crew. They made it sound like real James Bond stuff. You're supposed to carry on with your current mission, but I'm leaving to pick up another crew and plane."

By the time the sun was coming up, I had connected with another crew (who knew nothing!), settled into a new hotel, and waited. First thing in the morning, a diplomat from the State Department called us to the "secure room" next to ACP.

"This briefing is classified Secret NOFORN" (Not to be shared with representatives from foreign governments or militaries, hence "NO-Foreign"). President Nixon is traveling to Yalta to meet with Soviet leader Leonid Brezhnev. You are being tasked to fly the Secret Service and the White House Staff that are also going.

"Tensions are very high. You must be very careful. Everywhere you go, there will be spies, cameras, and microphones. You must not say anything about policy or tactics, and especially may not say anything about the contents of this mission or what I am briefing you. You must be on your guard. When you check into your hotel, you should anticipate a gorgeous KGB spy to try to meet you at a bar or knock on your hotel room door. They usually say something like, 'I am student and want to practice English—can I come in your room?'"

He continued, "This is a total set-up. They want to get in your room to put you in a compromising situation (which will be filmed with hidden cameras!) and used to blackmail you."

He went on to describe the sources of the tensions around the meeting, what the President planned to address, and what they were watching in other nations that had links to this trip in one way or another.

Several of the matters he briefed my new crew and me about were very significant. The most serious of them were news to all of us and involved some real cloak-and-dagger stuff that was directly related to what we were doing. So much so, the young lieutenant co-pilot on this new crew expressed his disdain by mocking what was said by our briefing officer.

I didn't know him or the other people on this new crew. They were assigned to fly the same kind of plane that I flew, but they were from a different base. They were all new to me. Still, I was surprised by the young co-pilot's attitude.

Just as we had been briefed, when we arrived at our plane, we were soon met by two Russian Air Force guys. One was a Navigator replete with faded Xerox copies of maps, and the other was a Radio Operator. The Soviet Union was the only country in the world that did not use English for Air Traffic Control. We had to have an interpreter along to translate.

Immediately, the Russian Navigator plopped down into the Nav seat and began throwing switches to program the navigation computers. Obviously, we were totally surprised by that.

"You seem to be pretty comfortable programming our Nav computers," I said.

He paused and grinned, and said in a very thick movie-style accent, "Vee are familiar."

Just as we had been briefed, the added Soviet crew members were obviously KGB spies.

On landing, as our CIA briefer had warned, agents latched onto us. They were never alone (they were watching each other), and we were never alone. One was a translator, and the other was—I suppose—a "watcher," someone put there to monitor us so we could not have any unauthorized contact with outsiders.

When we checked into the hotel, as the CIA agent had predicted, each of us had a beautiful KGB female agent show up at our hotel room door, hoping to seduce one of us into compromising behavior that could be used to blackmail us.

All those encounters made it very clear to me—and anyone else with sense—that this was a volatile situation with very dangerous security implications.

At dinner, they ushered us into a private dining room, insisting on which crew member sat in each seat. It was obvious that they were listening, recording, and probably filming everything we said or did. As a result, I was utterly shocked and amazed when the young copilot started talking about the classified CIA briefing we had received.

"Woah!" I turned to the lieutenant and said, "We are not to talk about that. Remember?"

With utter disdain, he rolled his eyes and smirked, making it obvious that he thought what we had been told about being spied upon was ridiculous.

A few minutes into conversation about other things, the young copilot *again* brought up the classified briefing. At this point, I was furious. I could actually feel my blood pressure rising, and my heart began to pound in my chest.

"I told you to stop!" And I glared at him.

Once again, he rolled his eyes and smirked, like I was an idiot and he knew best, but at least for the moment, he stopped talking. It wasn't long, though, before he started talking again about the sensitive classified briefing items. This time, he specifically referenced one of the most significant (and most secret) matters that we had been told before our flight.

At this point, I was not just angry, I was absolutely *furious*! My blood pressure shot up so much I actually saw the room with a red tint. [Later, a doctor told me that in situations of extreme stress, our blood pressure can skyrocket so much that the blood vessels in our eyes give a red tint to vision. That was what was happening!]

My anger was multifaceted. I was angry that he was disobeying how he had been told to comport himself. I was angry that he was actually endangering our mission—even our country. It's not likely that his indiscretion would actually tip some international balance the wrong way, but small things can have devastating effects. I was also angry that he was disregarding my instructions, and I was particularly peeved that he was acting badly with an extremely irritating smug smirk that was nauseating.

As I was processing things, I could feel myself toying with letting go and screaming at him. I had a strong urge to embarrass and humiliate him. Thankfully, the Holy Spirit was there, too, and nudged me to pause and take a breath.

I remembered my Grandfather talking about handling problem people under his command. In a fraction of a second, I was back with him as he was talking about taking a new command and finding that one of the people in the office had terrible body odor. In talking with others in the office, he learned that the situation had been going on for a very long time, actually through the tenure of several commanders.

The last solution that his predecessor tried was posting a list of expectations on the office bulletin board. It listed things that were expected of each person in the office. "Everyone is expected to be on time, and to come to the office well groomed." Obviously, that approach had not worked, and my grandfather inherited the challenge of dealing with the offending party.

"When there is a need to address a problem with an individual, attempting to finesse the problem with a new general rule for the whole unit instead of talking with the individual, is leadership cowardice," said Grandfather.

I knew that this situation was really serious and that how I handled it was going to be important. I closed my eyes and retreated into imagining looking into the face of Jesus. In my mind's eye, what I saw surprised me. There was a compassionate face of Jesus, somehow not minimizing this young arrogant pilot's foolish mistake and the danger it was bringing, but at the same time, showing the broken side of this young man and his need for correction that was not destructive, but redemptive. As is often the case with Jesus, He offers a surprising re-interpretation of how we see things. In this case, I was aware that He was giving me what I needed to deal with the situation, but He also wanted me to care compassionately for the young pilot. That didn't mean I wouldn't be tough, but it did mean that I would not be destructive.

> *From the General:*
> When there is a need to address a problem with an individual, attempting to finesse the problem with a new general rule for the whole unit instead of talking with the individual is leadership cowardice.
> — Brig. Gen. James A. Pickering

I knew that this situation was really serious and that how I handled it was going to be important. I closed my eyes and retreated into imagining looking into the face of Jesus. In my mind's eye, what I saw surprised me. There was a compassionate face of Jesus, but I still felt He was calling me to correct the problem.

As I calmed, I knew I had to say something to him without flying off the handle. I breathed in slowly, and as I did so, I could feel my heart slowing. It was as though the Lord was assuring me that He would give me the words to say — and convey them with sufficient authority to halt this impending disaster. I needed to fix this situation and make him *stop*.

"Listen, lieutenant," I said in a measured voice but with a grave tone, "I know that you think that this is ridiculous, but at this point, I have to protect not only our mission, but I need to protect you from yourself. What you are doing is incredibly foolish. You must stop what you are doing. I am now giving you a direct order, as your superior officer, to stop this. You may not refer to anything sensitive or classified. If you violate this direct order, I assure you that on our return, I will file court-martial charges against you and do everything in my power to have you prosecuted and punished. You may think that, too, is ridiculous, but

I assure you that your Commander will not. You will now stop this, period."

He had stopped talking but was glaring at me with a menacing look. Before long, he reached out and grabbed a small flower vase from the middle of the table and pulled it toward himself like it was a microphone.

Defiantly, he spoke into the flowers. "Excuse me, we need some butter out here. Could you bring us some more butter?" and continued glaring at me.

Without any delay at all, in just a few seconds the kitchen door swung open and a waiter came out with a butter dish on a tray. The waiter, with a ceremonious flourish, dramatically placed the butter dish directly in front of the copilot—and smiled at him.

To be honest, I couldn't tell if the waiter was a KGB operative showing off, or a "regular guy" who was warning us that we were under surveillance. In any case, the butter-delivering waiter re-interpreted the scene by affirming that it was a dangerous environment.

I looked at the young copilot's face. It was drained and completely white. He was shocked and terrified and realized that he had made an awful mistake.

He turned toward me and said contritely, "I'm sorry! I'm sorry! I'm *so* sorry!"

"It's OK," I replied. "Just stay in your lane now moving forward."

"Yes, sir," came the meek reply.

This incident illustrates the importance of waiting on the Lord before reacting to someone or some situation in anger. When I retreated into my relationship with Jesus before addressing the young man, His presence brought a sweet sense of calm. In my mind's eye, I could see Jesus' face. His expression didn't minimize the seriousness of the situation, but His look was filled simultaneously with understanding for my predicament and with compassion for the young pilot. I could not have imagined that balance on my own. I would have leaned toward either compassion or addressing the situation.

As I experienced the presence of Jesus, my anger faded, and I was able to respond to the situation much more calmly. It is fascinating, however, that redirecting events became much easier with the intervention of the waiter. He was a big help by being present and making clear that we could protect ourselves and stop things from moving further in a dark direction.

With the powerful emotion of anger, we are aware that there is something that we want to stop. It is painful, frightening, unpleasant, and negative in many more ways. Our need is two-fold. First, we want whatever is negative to stop, but secondly, we need relationships so we can recapture joy. Remember that joy resides (the "joy center") in the fourth level of the brain, the prefrontal cortex. In order to recapture joy from anger, we must be able to attune with someone in order for our cingulate cortex to be activated and so it "lights up." It is in that circumstance that our brain and its associated chemicals release joy again.

To recapture joy from anger, you can find your own pathway, but what I have discovered as a way to do so.

First of all, Jesus knows that life in this fallen world will sometimes result in our getting angry. How we handle it is what is important.

> *Be angry but do not sin; do not let the sun go down on your anger, and do not make room for the devil. (Ephesians 4:26-27)*

This Scripture tells us that God knows that there are going to be things that make us angry, but we should not dwell on them. Anger is poisonous to us if we hold on to it. When people cling to anger, at the end of the day, there is a release of the chemical cortisol. It has the effect of washing through the brain and removing whatever accumulation of joy has been built up in the cingulate cortex.[29] As a result, we should be highly motivated to resolve anger issues.

The heart of anger is the feeling in adverse circumstances that I need to protect myself. For me, the heart of returning to joy from anger is getting in touch with the Lord and experiencing His presence and promise that He will protect me.

> *You who live in the shelter of the Most High,*
> *who abide in the shadow of the Almighty,*
> *will say to the LORD, "My refuge and my fortress;*
> *my God, in whom I trust."*

---

[29] Leggett AN, Zarit SH, Kim K, Almeida DM, Klein LC. (2015) Depressive mood, anger, and daily cortisol of caregivers on high- and low-stress days," J Gerontol B Psychol Sci Soc Sci 70(6):820-9.

For he will deliver you from the snare of the fowler
*   and from the deadly pestilence;*
he will cover you with his pinions,
*   and under his wings you will find refuge;*
*   His faithfulness is a shield and buckler.*
You will not fear the terror of the night,
*   or the arrow that flies by day,*
or the pestilence that stalks in darkness,
*   or the destruction that wastes at noonday.*
A thousand may fall at your side,
*   ten thousand at your right hand,*
*   but it will not come near you. (Psalm 91:1-7)*

I have found that meditating on that Psalm gives me a sense of security that the Lord is my protector, and I can rest in Him.

Chapter 12
Recapturing Joy from SHAME

I'm not bringing you joy and/or <u>you are not glad to be with me.</u>

Shame is entirely relational, on the right side of the brain. We feel shame in our relationship either with another person or with God. When we violate our own internal moral compass and depart from our own values, we can actually feel shame towards ourselves as well. There is no joy when I am feeling shame, and I am aware that there is another person (or a group of people) who is not glad to be with me. It is far worse than loneliness. The bond and the presence of the other person (or people) is excruciating rather than joy-producing.

There are two basic types of shame. One is called *healthy shame* and the other is *toxic shame*. In healthy shame, we are learning the values of the community of which we are a part. Instructions such as "Don't chew with your mouth open" or "Close the bathroom door!" help us learn the cultural rhythm and expectations of "our people."

Toxic shame usually rises from thoughts in our left brain. It occurs when we violate relational trust and find ourselves interpreting the internal or relational tension, and it feels terrible. To quiet ourselves and return to joy from shame, we need to have a relationship with someone (another person or Jesus) with whom we have confidence that the relationship will endure and will not be dissolved. The security that someone is glad to be with me even in the midst of a serious problem is a starting point. Peace can grow from that secure place of attunement with that person.

Experiencing shame is awful. Here's an example from my own life.

People had come from all over the U.S. and Canada, not to mention many other nations, to gather for a conference on Hope in the midst of the spiritual devastation that was coming to the Episcopal church after the leadership had departed from Biblical authority. I had spent the ten years leading up to this conference flying all over the world networking Anglican Archbishops to work for the re-establishment of Biblical authority in the Episcopal Church. It started off with my asking them for help because I saw how weak the leaders in the Episcopal Church were. It wasn't long before a group of Archbishops invited me to leave parish ministry and go to work for them, traveling among them and updating them on each other's plans and concerns. I traveled around the world time and time again, meeting with each one and going on to the next. During the decade leading up to the conference, I had traveled literally millions of miles networking with the Archbishops and serving their leadership vision. My connections had been rich and rewarding. The Archbishops were not just bosses, they were dear friends. Our relationships had grown deep and strong—at least that's what I thought!

For this U.S. conference, I had been asked to be the host on the platform, introducing Archbishops who were speaking and helping to provide links to segue from one topic to the next. Then, on the morning of the conference, the organizing Bishop pulled me aside and said, "I have to remove you from conference leadership. I have been told that you have seriously offended The Primates (the Archbishops in charge of nations or groups of nations), and I have heard that they are refusing to work with you anymore. I can't have you on the platform."

It was a total shock, and it was devastating. I could feel my face red and my ears burning hot with shame. My mind was spinning with confusion. I wasn't aware of any conflict or disappointment from the Primates.

Fortunately, my grandfather had much earlier given me a principle upon which to lean. To the young man, now grown and confused, the General had said, "When you are reading a map—or navigating life—it is critically important to know where you actually are even if it is bad news. You need to know so you can chart where you need to go.

From the General:
When you are reading a map—or navigating life—it is critically important to know where you actually are even if it is bad news. You need to know so you can chart where you need to go.
--Brig. Gen. James A. Pickering

I knew what I had to do. I went back to the hotel where the Archbishops were staying and knocked on the door of one of them. He welcomed me warmly and invited me into his room to talk. Recounting the conversation I had just had, and the fact that I had been fired from being the Master of Ceremonies for the conference, I asked him what he had heard.

"Absolutely nothing. I've heard nothing! In fact, you always serve us with distinction. Something is amiss. Let me get in touch with the organizer and see if I can sort this out."

He picked up the phone in the room, called the organizing Bishop, and asked what was going on.

Of course, I could only hear his side of the conversation, but I could hear how supportive he was. He remarked into the phone, "You have been misinformed. Bill is not only our colleague but our friend. Someone has given you bad information."

When he finished the phone call, he hung up and turned to me, "Well, he is not backing down from his decision to remove you, but at least now we know what is going on. I found out who told him this erroneous information."

He named another pastor who was very competitive and jealous of the relationship that I had with the Archbishops. He wanted to be connected with them. Apparently, he figured that if he got me removed, it would enhance his stature with the Archbishops.

Although I now had a better idea of what was going on, dealing with it was still very hard. I couldn't announce that I had been unjustly removed and that the report was false. It was one of those unfair happenings in life. At least I knew that the Archbishops weren't mad at me.

Although I now had a better idea of what was going on, dealing with it was still very hard. I couldn't announce that I had been unjustly removed and that the report was false. It was one of those unfair happenings in life. At least I knew that the Archbishops weren't mad at me. This Archbishop's willingness to stay connected to me made matters bearable, even though the situation was still awful and humiliating—especially because everyone knew that I was supposed to be the Master of Ceremonies. Later, as the conference started, I took a seat in the middle of the auditorium. I could still feel the sting of shame.

The heart of shame is *I'm not bringing you joy and/or you are not glad to be with me.*

That was a perfect description of the situation with the organizing Bishop of the conference. He was certainly not glad to be with me. That was so true that he ordered me off the platform.

When the conference started, the giant convention center auditorium was packed. The program unfolded with Archbishops being introduced and having a number of people speak. Then, the conversation turned to thanking and affirming people who had been battling faithfully for Biblical authority. One person after another was recognized, with their contributions being lauded. The love fest went on for more than an hour, all of it led by the organizing Bishop. My "friend" who had wrongly accused me and lied about my standing with the Archbishops, proudly sat in my seat on the platform, smiling broadly throughout. When he was recognized, he feigned embarrassment and shook his head "No," but it was pretty obvious, given the circumstances, that he was reveling in his moment.

Sitting there watching the mockery, I thought I was alone, and, yet, Scripture tells us that Jesus completely understood my betrayal and the shame I was experiencing. Had He not experienced so much more, with the betrayal of his disciples, all of whom deserted Him, and then standing before Pilate, falsely accused and yet refusing to defend Himself? We are told by the writer to the Hebrews that Jesus has gone before us in all circumstances:

> *For we do not have a high priest who is unable to sympathize with our weaknesses, but we have one who was tempted [tested] in every way that we are, yet was without sin. Let us then approach the throne of grace with confidence so that we may receive mercy and find grace to help us in our time of need. (Hebrews 4:15, 16)*

As this was going on, I realized that I had to make a choice. Several of them in fact. First, I had to deal with the shame I was feeling. Second, I had to forgive my colleague who had so terribly and falsely betrayed me. I elected to do both.

Thanking Jesus for redemption, I said, "Lord, I give you the situation and the shame. I ask you to wash over it and bear fruit at this meeting. Don't let the misdeeds of my colleague rob the spiritual fruit you desire to bring here. Secondly, please don't hold this sin against him. Forgive him, Lord, and help me to forgive him totally and completely."

Just as I finished praying those two things, the pastor who was sitting next to me turned and said, "I just realized something. With all those that they are recognizing and thanking, why aren't you up there. All of this is because of what you have done. Why aren't you being thanked?"

"I didn't do anything for recognition," I said. "Everything has been done for the Lord."

At that moment, a flood of the Holy Spirit washed over me. I could sense the Lord's presence loving me. It was amazing, concrete, and exhilarating. Then came the best part. He spoke to me—not out loud, but with clear, distinct words. He said, "For this cause," I knew He meant how I had handled this problem, "In the Kingdom, I am promoting you in the Spirit. You have handled this well and I am pleased with you."

I was elated. My "friend" who had betrayed me had meant this for ill, but God had just turned it for good! It was an amazing feeling. Instead of shame, I knew that the Lord knew the truth. I felt a flood of peace. Amazingly, the situation had not changed. I was still sitting in the congregation and was not recognized in the parade of those being thanked, but I didn't care. I knew the Lord's favor. That was worth much more than the praise of men. Another thing. I knew that what my "friend" had done, while meant to remove me, had actually led to an increase of favor and anointing. I realized that if I could reach him, I would throw my arms around him and give him a hug and a kiss. He had gotten me promoted in the Kingdom. At that point, I didn't even know what that would look like, but I knew it would be good!

It had been a huge help that the Archbishop with whom I spoke had been clear that his care for me had not been diminished by the charge that I had done something wrong. At some deep level, I even knew that if there were a real problem (rather than a manufactured false one), he would still be glad to be in relationship with me. He exhibited true brotherly companionship. It was not based on perfect performance; it was based on a powerful covenant. In human terms, he demonstrated the way that the Lord loves us!

When we are confronted with situations like this one, which cause embarrassment and shame, we need to remember that the Lord has purpose in them. How we respond will determine whether we stay in that shame, deserved or undeserved, and thereby allow it to consume us, or invoke the promise of Romans 8:28: "All things work together for good, to those who love the Lord, to those who are called according to His purpose." This is a good verse to use to start the process of "quieting" ourselves.

In recapturing joy from shame, here is what I have discovered:

- Make sure relational circuits are on.
- Turn to Jesus for quieting.
- Tap into a supportive connection with another person (human or Jesus).

- Recall Scriptural promises in which you can hear the voice of the Lord (or the other person) showing you how to change your perspective.
- Listen to the voice of the Lord sharing that He is glad to be with you. .

To know that Jesus is glad to be with me, I need look no further than this verse from Hebrews:

> *...looking to Jesus the pioneer and perfecter of our faith, who for the sake of the joy that was set before him endured the cross, disregarding its shame, and has taken his seat at the right hand of the throne of God. (Hebrews 12:2)*

The great encouragement to me is knowing that I am the joy that motivated Jesus to endure the Cross. I revisit a quiet and gentle place in my mind and heart where I have previously experienced His grace, recall the verse from Hebrews, and ask Him what He would like to say. The results have been truly amazing. Again and again, I have been bathed in His love and acceptance, knowing His joy at being with me.

Chapter 13
Recapturing Joy from DISGUST

That is <u>not life-giving</u>!

When we are experiencing the powerful emotion of disgust, we have a *huge* joy disruptor. The underlying concept is that the circumstances are not "life giving," but it is much more powerful than those words convey to me. Disgust is gut-wrenching. It is horrible, stomach churning, and revolting. In a word, it is disgusting!

In order to quiet from disgust, we must have a way of returning to life. There must be a way that we can experience cleansing. As we are "washed" (at least figuratively!), the washing gives us a new place to stand where we can escape the disgust we have been feeling. To recapture our joy means that we must navigate through event(s) or circumstance(s) that may well still be present, but we come to a place where we have dominion over them. Instead of allowing disgusting things to overwhelm us, we stand over them.

In my ministry as a Bishop, I'm responsible for overseeing clergy. Usually, that is a great joy, allowing me to coach and encourage faithful and gifted, godly people. Other times, however, there is a need for correction and even discipline, and they may cause me disgust.

One such instance began when my phone rang one evening. I didn't recognize the number, but I recognized the voice immediately. It was the wife of one of the pastors I oversee. I could tell from the quiver in her voice that she was really upset.

"Bishop, I am at my wit's end." Obviously crying, she said, "I've found hundreds of text messages on my husband's phone to a woman he has known since high school. He has told her that we have been separated for more than a year, and our divorce is almost final. As you know, we have not been separated, and there hasn't been any discussion of divorce! The messages say that he is planning to go to the town where she lives to spend the weekend with her. I took pictures of the messages, and I can send them to you."

I tried to help her calm, and prayed with her, but the situation was anguishing and . . . .horrible.

Because I was responsible for oversight of this pastor, I had to look at this evidence. It certainly wasn't because I had any desire to do so. When the email with all the "screenshots" of the text messages arrived, my questions morphed into disgust, as the certainty of the situation was laid bare. Then, as I read more and more, I saw instance after instance of betrayal. I read concrete evidence that contradicted things that he had been telling me. He had protested for months about how he was seeking help to enrich his marriage, but the messages showed he had been plotting an affair in a devastatingly calculated way. The more I read, the more I realized the seriousness of the situation, and it actually evoked a feeling of nausea.

The role of the pastor is one of deep spiritual responsibility. Instead, this pastor had exhibited duplicitous premeditated betrayal of his wife, family, the congregation, me (as his bishop), and, worst of all, the Lord. The vortex of what should have been godly, righteous behavior and sacrificial family leadership was swirling around a snake pit of lies. What arose in me was extreme disgust.

The classic definition of disgust is "That is not life-giving!" In this case, the information I was reading definitely was not life-giving. In fact, it was very much the opposite. This was life-destroying.

While reading the various lies, I felt revulsion that churned in my gut. It was the sour stomach one gets after having consumed curdled milk. I could feel the rise of tension, especially with my shoulders tightening. The lump in my gut was worsening as I realized I couldn't just end my relationship with him and walk away. I was going to have to deal with something that was very serious, that was exactly the *opposite* of life-giving. And I had to do it with sensitivity to his family, not to mention all the people who attended the church.

My stomach was so upset, I actually thought I was going to vomit, but I knew that the first order of business was to retreat into the Lord and get myself settled down – to quiet.

I decided to call the pastor who was the errant pastor's ministry supervisor. I had spoken with him several times, but today I wanted to brainstorm with the supervisor about how to proceed. On the phone, instead of offering solutions, the other pastor (one I also supervise) was extremely helpful and affirming.

"This is an awful situation," he said. "I can't imagine the pressures you have, being responsible for situations like this. I can tell you, however, that I am completely confident that you will handle it well."

That was an amazing affirmation, and helped me settle and regain perspective. The input of another person with whom we can attune empowers us to move forward.

As I prayed for the Lord's help, He immediately answered my prayer with a very clear picture of the Grand Canyon. Even without words from Him I could see why He was showing it to me. There was a great chasm between God and me. Somehow, I knew that the important task facing me was to get to the other side of the canyon—to get to where the Father was, where I could experience His love. It was a picture of the heart of what we might call "the religious quest." It is the burning human desire and need to get fellowship and intimacy with God restored.

In my mind's eye, it was like the Lord was playing a movie for me. I could see people lining up to try to jump across the canyon. Some were not athletic at all and fell to the canyon floor almost immediately after jumping. Others were more athletic, and less morally compromised. When they jumped, they were able to travel through the air much farther than most—certainly much farther than I—before they plunged to the canyon floor. The scene was quite comical, reminding me of the cartoon character Wile E Coyote, the ill-fated cartoon pursuer of the Road Runner. Constantly confounded in his efforts to catch the bird, Wile E Coyote would regularly fall to the bottom of a canyon in a cloud of dust and a "poof." I could feel the failure of not having the means to get across the canyon in my own strength as I saw my ignominious failure leading to perishing in my own moral fall.

From the General:
All authority comes from God.
-- Brig. Gen. James A. Pickering

In the midst of that, I "heard" the voice of the Lord speaking. "Everyone needs my grace." As soon as I heard them, those words resulted in a flood of forgiveness. It was a tide of grace that rolled over me, highlighting my own vulnerabilities. It did not say I could overlook the terrible behavior of the pastor, but it did help me see my own shortcomings, so that the discipline I had to mete out would be done in love rather than with indignation.

Without a question, the image that the Lord gave me caused my disgust to melt into compassion. The tension faded, and I realized that my stomach was peaceful. Once again, Jesus had gifted me with His peace! I still had to bring discipline to the leader who had acted out so terribly, but I could do it now with a softer heart. It is always bad when people make bad moral choices, but it is devastating when those kinds of bad choices are made by someone in leadership. The abuse of authority had to be addressed and order restored, or the whole community would be assaulted by the toxicity. In that moment, I was reminded of the wise words my grandfather had spoken to me years earlier: "All authority comes from God." Abusing authority was, in essence, going against God, not me.

When I arranged to speak with the errant pastor, I tried to set him up for redemption. I invited him to tell me about his marriage, hoping he would be honest about the real issues.

When I arranged to speak with the errant pastor, I tried to set him up for redemption. I invited him to tell me about his marriage, hoping he would be honest about the real issues. Sadly, he was not forthcoming, but wove a tale of lies. I was able to challenge him with the truth, telling him I had seen his text messages. Thankfully, his response was, "Oh. You know. I have made a complete mess of my life. Tell me what to do. I don't know what to do anymore. I will do whatever you say." We were then able to begin a healing process, for him, his wife, and all involved. My change in attitude did not diminish the seriousness of his offenses, but it paved the path to bring life-giving aid to a situation that was wrought with life-destroying potential.

Of course, we cannot know what might have happened had the Lord not softened my angered (and disgusted) heart, but I'm pretty sure that it would have been very destructive.

In recapturing joy from disgust, here is what I have discovered; knowing Jesus, and knowing that He is the Life-giver changes my heart!

> *In the beginning was the Word, and the Word was with God, and the Word was God. He was in the beginning with God. All things were made through Him, and without Him nothing was made that was made. In Him was life, and the life was the light of men. (John 1:1-4)*

At its heart, disgust is the negative awareness that something we are experiencing is not life-giving. For me, recovering from that feeling centers around an experience with another person, or Jesus Himself, that is profoundly life-giving. That He is The Life Giver of John Chapter 1 is a wonderful place to begin.

Chapter 14
Recapturing Joy from FEAR

Fear carries the powerful feeling that I want to get away from something.

The feeling that "I want to get away" from something or someone is a primal response to avoid being hurt, or even killed. The problem is that we cannot always actually get away! We need to learn to *be quiet* in the face of that which causes us fear. That is certainly not easy, but it is something that can be learned.

When I was a young boy, I was being bullied by some other children. I desperately wanted to get away from them. When I arrived at home, my Grandfather was there as usual. He could see that I was really distressed, exceedingly so. He knew that I had been crying. Without a word, he motioned me over to him as he sat on a big chair, and calmly lifted me onto his lap—just like he had done many times before, he silently drew me into a very tight hug. He slowly and gently breathed in and out until I was echoing his breathing pattern. I could feel his warmth, and I knew that he was a safe place and that I was loved. Now, I didn't want to get away. I wanted to stay right there. I can remember my hand on his chest, feeling the fabric of his old army shirt. It was a bit frayed, but clean and stiff. Even though he had retired from the service and wasn't using it as an Army uniform any more, old habits die slowly. He would usually wear the old uniform shirts—still insisting that they were starched stiff as a board. I can even remember the many times that I took his starched old uniform shirts off the rack where they were hung and stood them up on the floor like little short persons with super long arms and no legs. To me, the shirts epitomized his military bearing and security.

As I sat in his lap, my heart began to calm. Holding me as he did caused me to sync with him, and I began to receive his peace. Even before he spoke, his physical presence was so powerful, I began to be flooded with confidence that I could have victory over the circumstances around my life that were so upsetting. I realized that I was not alone, and I no longer wanted to get away.

While I was syncing with him, he asked me what had caused me to be upset. As I told him about the other children circling me and bullying me, and how that made me afraid, he pulled me even tighter. That embrace called me to peace, and I could feel my heart rate slowing. My head was on his chest, and I could feel his calm and steady heartbeat. I felt the corners of my mouth begin to turn up into a smile.

The bullies had not disappeared. In fact, there was no other way back to my house from the nearby playground that didn't pass through "their turf." I knew I was going to have to face them again and again. He knew that too. He knew that the best way forward was not for him to go scorch the earth on them because this was only one negative situation. There would be many more.

As he held me, I could feel his solution rising. He was going to equip me for the circumstance: changing *me*, instead of changing the environment. "Remember this," he said, "...a hardboiled egg is *always* yellow inside." I was used to his talking to me like that--using simile and metaphor. I knew what he was telling me. He meant that bullies always had a cowardly heart inside. It was cowardice, not power, that motivated them. I felt a flood of peace and confidence. Somehow, he had shown me that the solution to my fear was not getting away from it but overcoming it--standing up to the bullies. The funny way he had spoken somehow gave me complete confidence that the bullies were paper tigers that would fold if I stood up to them. Even before it all played out, he had equipped me to stand in the midst of fear. He made me a better person, simply by drawing me to himself and giving me a fresh insight about what was true and real.

> From the General:
> ...a hardboiled egg is *always* yellow inside.
> -- Brig. Gen. James A. Pickering

The amazing thing about transforming love is that it changes us even if the circumstances don't change. After being loved by my Grandfather to stillness inside, the next time I had to go through the bullies' neighborhood, it was different. When I approached, they looked the same, but I saw them differently.

As they came toward me with their smirks and insults, they were confident that they were going to be able to torment me again. This time, it was different. I had been loved into more wholeness than I had before. The key to recovery from fear is bonding with a person who can help us calm and whose presence gives us security that is distinct from that which causes us fear. This can be either a regular human with whom we have a relationship, or it can be accomplished with our bonds with Jesus.

Watching them approach, I knew that they were "hard boiled eggs," and they were "yellow inside." I remember actually smiling. As they got close, I stood with my feet planted (just like I had seen my Grandfather do!) and faced them squarely. As they came nearer, I held up my hand with two fingers crooked just like Grandfather did, and said, "Don't!" Then with complete confidence (because in my experience my Grandfather was *never* wrong!) I said, "I will hurt you."

They stopped and looked shocked. Then the leader, the one who had tormented me the most, turned and walked away saying, "Let's get out of here!"

They never bothered me again. Thanks to my Grandfather's transforming love, I no longer wanted to flee. He had helped me triumph, prevailing over the circumstances rather than being overwhelmed by them.

My Grandfather continued to have a huge influence on my life. By the time I was in college, I only lived about five houses from his house, and I saw him all the time. When college calculus baffled me, he said, "Here," grabbing a pad of paper and a pencil, "Calculus is simple. Imagine that you shoot an artillery shell from a howitzer," and drew a curve across the pad. "The arc that the shell takes is a curve. Imagine that you put a rod up in the shape of the curve. Now, from that rod, you want to hang a curtain. Calculus is just the way to figure out how much material you will need for the curtain." He went on to explain it so clearly, I actually did well in that class!

> *Jesus draws us close, loves us into more wholeness, and then reinterprets the world for us so it is defined by Him rather than by circumstances.*

At that time, he was 77 years old but still was sharp as a tack!

Later, I would come to know that my grandfather's love that changed me time and time again is the way that Jesus Christ works in our lives. Jesus draws us close, loves us into more wholeness, and then reinterprets the world for us so it is defined by Him rather than by circumstances.

In the case of recapturing joy from fear, here is what I have discovered:
- Make sure relational circuits are on.
- Turn to Jesus for quieting.
- Tap into a supportive connection with another person (human or Jesus).

- Listen to the voice of the Lord (or the other person) showing you how to change your perspective.
- Listen for insight into the situation.
- Act on that insight to either be changed or to get away.
- Use Scripture to dispel the fear.

Of the negative emotions, fear seems to be the strongest for me. Part of that may be that I have had so many experiences where the consequences I feared were of great magnitude, but in any case, fear can be very challenging to deal with. There are many Scriptural promises that encourage us not to live in fear. For example:

> *Do not fear, for I am with you,*
>   *do not be afraid, for I am your God;*
> *I will strengthen you, I will help you,*
>   *I will uphold you with my victorious right hand. (Isaiah 41:10)*

And...

> *He has said, "I will never leave you or forsake you."*
> *So we can say with confidence,*
> *"The Lord is my helper; I will not be afraid.*
> *What can anyone do to me?" (Hebrews 13:5b-6)*

For some, after quieting, meditating on those promises might be enough. For me, it is helpful to return to a safe and quiet place with the Lord and ask Him to speak to me.

For many years, that place for me has been to visualize the face of Aslan, the Type of Christ found in C.S. Lewis', *Chronicles of Narnia*. As I welcome Him, it is as though He comes and presses His forehead against mine. In that place, I can sense His pleasure of being with me. When I ask Him what He would like to say to me, He seems to always respond with lovely, surprising affirmations.

In that place, He makes real the Scripture:

> *You show me the path of life.*
> *In your presence there is fullness of joy;*
> *in your right hand are pleasures forevermore. (Psalm 16:11)*

Again and again, I have seen Him melt my fear and turn it into joy to be with Him, even in the midst of terrible circumstances. It is not necessarily the case that He makes the problem go away, He can change me in the midst of the circumstances.

Chapter 15
The Prefrontal Cortex – True Identity

Who am I? Who are my people? How should I act?

Earlier, I wrote about how Attachment, Assessment, and Attunement work together to present subconscious information to Level Four, the Prefrontal Cortex of the right hemisphere. It is in this place that we assemble understanding about our True Identity, subconsciously. In other words, we have a clear identity that guides our sense of who we are, but it has been formed "under the table" (i.e., beneath our conscious understanding). My true identity not only concerns who I am, but also has a community aspect. We might describe that aspect as "Who are my people?"

My "tribe" is composed of the ones with whom I live and move. The corporate identity we have formed together is tremendously defining. The process involves the way that the right hemisphere of the brain handles information. As experiences are "coded" as good, bad, or scary, the ones that are labeled as good have an attendant feel-good chemical wash impact the neural pathways. The main chemical released in this circumstance is dopamine. It is complex, but apparently, dopamine can also be released in circumstances of pain, which may help explain somewhat how addictions develop.

"It appears from our study that dopamine acts as an interface between stress, pain and emotions, or between physical and emotional events, and that it's activated with both positive and negative stimuli...[30]In terms of establishing identity, the pathways that have been bathed in dopamine during "good" experiences with others, develop a neural pathway that builds a link with the memory of the other person. The activity and the person are assembled in the Prefrontal Cortex (PFC) as "my people" and "how we act in this given circumstance."

The development of who "my people" are, is more challenging in Western cultures than it is in some others of the global South. Although

---

[30] "Pleasure And Pain: Study Shows Brain's 'Pleasure Chemical' Is Involved In Response To Pain Too." ScienceDaily. ScienceDaily, 19 October 2006. Review of Scott DJ, Heitzeg MM, Koeppe RA, Stohler CS, Zubieta J-K. (2006) Variations in the human pain stress experience mediated by ventral and dorsal basal ganglia dopamine activity. J Neurosci 26(42):10789-95.

many people think that tribal cultures in Africa, for example, are undeveloped and primitive, one need only look at some of their core beliefs about community to see how healthy and sophisticated some of those tribal identities are.

For example, in Western Europe and America, Descartes' treatise *Cogito ergo sum* ("I think therefore I am") sums up the perspective held by many people with regard to the world. It is supremely individualistic. By contrast, in both East and West Africa, I have had the great opportunity to work with many different tribes including Igbo, Kikuyu, Luhya, Kalenjin, Luo, Kamba, and Maasai. Despite the many differences among the tribes, people from all of those tribes would often speak of the philosophy, "I am because we are." They are well aware of the essential nature of being connected with "my people," and celebrating that link. We have a lot to learn from them! They understand our interconnections far better than we. Neurologically, we are designed to link and sync with other people.[31] The ones with whom we link are considered "our people." Experiencing what they think and do shapes our identity and behavior profoundly.

As we attach with other people with whom we have formed meaningful bonds, new neural pathways are established in our brains. Basically, that just means that our brain records the relationships and experiences. As we attune with other people's brains, we create a mutual mind state that shares brain matter "lighting up" in the same places in both our brain and the other person's. We can develop profound and joyful connections with others. It is these with whom we have connected who relationally become "My people." This "linking" is all subconscious, however. We can have a sense of bonding with them, but "brain-wise," it is just a sense of belonging.

Time spent sharing attunement in the midst of other experiences can fuel our feelings of connection. We begin to know the norms of our "community," and they resonate deeply within us and guide our actions. These bonds provide strong guidance. They may not be conscious, but they are powerful.

As my brain begins to articulate this identity, it passes a systematic worldview from the right hemisphere of my brain to the left hemisphere. Long before my conscious thoughts awaken to the circumstances around me, my right hemisphere has figured out where I am and has sent a

---

[31] Siegel. *Developing Mind. op. cit.*, p. 2.

"therefore..." message to my conscious thoughts in my left hemisphere that all but constrains my actions.

In the earlier chapters in which I wrote about how to recapture joy, I was dealing with how we are settling down in the midst of troubling negative emotions. In this next section, we will look at another but very similar maturity skill: being able to act like our true self even in the midst of the six major negative emotions. Acting like ourselves is a maturity skill that bears tremendous fruit. When we do it properly, we value both our relationships and our goals, and what we experience is tremendously satisfying. Satisfaction is one of the profound desires of the human heart. Less than acquiring stuff, true satisfaction comes when we give and serve.

When we are assaulted by negative emotions, rather than escaping from them, the critical skill to learn is how to act like myself while in the midst of a negative emotion.

The approaches to recovering from negative emotions are a bit different from each other because the brain handles each of the major negative emotions in a slightly different way depending on which emotion is involved.[32]

Earlier, we were looking at recapturing joy from the six major negative emotions. We are also called to act like ourselves in the midst of those same emotions. We not only need to quiet, we also need to be able to function, and we need to be able to do so while the negative emotion is still present.

Acting like myself has several powerful aspects. First of all, being true to my identity is satisfying. Costly fidelity is immensely fulfilling. Second, the healthy person will want to pursue decisions and behaviors that are good for the whole community. Acting like one's true self not only will be personally fulfilling, but also will add to the joy base of the community. Acting like one's true self is also the best way to experience peace—at least in the long run.

The writer to the Hebrews says of Jesus:

> . . . looking unto Jesus, the author and finisher of our faith, who <u>for the joy that was set before Him</u> endured the cross, despising the shame, and has sat down at the right hand of the throne of God. (Hebrews 12:12; emphasis added)

---

[32] Dolan, Raymond. *The Anatomy of Fear*, https://www.humboldt-foundation.de/web/678825.html

Jesus knew that although there was pain to be endured at the Cross, doing it would bring joy. In this case, "the joy set before Him" is YOU! He went to the Cross in order to share its virtues and victories with you!!

In this next section, we will look at ways that acting like yourself is the best and most rewarding course.

Chapter 16
Acting Like My True Self in DESPAIR

The Bishop of Enugu, Nigeria, had invited me to Good Shepherd Cathedral to lead a retreat for his clergy and those from eight surrounding dioceses. The Eastern part of Nigeria is called Igboland (for the name of the majority tribe there, the Igbos [pronounced EE-bo; the g is silent]). In order to return to the United States, I had to go from the airport for internal domestic flights to the Murtala Mohammed International Airport. The airports are not far apart, but the trip is dangerous. I knew there were many stories of people hiring a taxi to take them from one airport to the other and never arriving. Many had been robbed and killed.

Knowing how dangerous things were, I had arranged for a friend to meet me at the domestic airport and take me to the international airport for my flight to Europe and then home. I was on high alert, even before I left the domestic terminal.

As I walked down the corridor, I saw two groups of three people I took to be plain-clothed police. Presumably, because I stood out as a foreigner, they must have thought I was vulnerable, or a likely source for getting bribery money. In any event, they quickly targeted me and made a circle around me, demanding to see my passport.

Upon seeing my visa, the first one shouted, "This visa is not valid! You are here in this country illegally!"

It was a standard ruse that I had heard many times before. At first, I was only mildly concerned because I had passed through similar attempts to extract bribery money from me, but this encounter turned very dark and very bad very quickly. One of them snatched my passport from my hand and stepped back as the others maintained a circle around me. One thing I knew in Africa. One does not want to be separated from one's passport! The one with my passport took several steps away, looking as if he were going to leave with it. At this point, I had not said anything.

Trying to defuse the situation, I said to them, "My visa was issued by your embassy in Washington, D.C. I'm sure they took good care to do it properly."

I suppose I was trying to apply the advise my Grandfather had once given me with regard to handling dangerous situations. He had said, "When you need to traverse a ridgeline, don't walk along the top of it. Walk down below the summit eight or ten feet. If you are on the top, you are silhouetted and are an easy target against the sky for enemy fire. There is always a way through where you need to go."

> *From the General:*
>
> When you need to traverse a ridgeline, don't walk along the top of it. Walk down below the summit eight or ten feet. If you are on the top, you are silhouetted and are an easy target against the sky for enemy fire. There is always a way through where you need to go.
>
> -- Brig. Gen. James A. Pickering

"Quiet!" they cried. "You are in this country illegally!"

Not only that, but two of them grabbed me...one on each arm with vice-like grips. I was startled at the violence of their grip. They held me with such strength that I was sure both arms were going to have bruises.

By this time, a significant crowd had gathered to watch what was happening. There were many people, circling in an arc around to the right, something like a half-circle.

The one with my passport began walking away.

The others who gripped me started pulling me in the opposite direction, saying, "We are taking you to jail!"

"Stop!" I said. "Give me back my passport."

I could feel the adrenalin rising and my heart rate going through the roof. My mouth was dry, and I saw this was going very badly.

"We are not giving you anything!" screamed the one on my right—probably trying to intimidate me with his shouting.

He had been gripping my right arm with his left hand on my bicep. His fingers dug into my arm deeply. It was really painful. From there, it got astronomically worse. While one gripped my right arm tightly with his left hand, and his partner gripped my left with an equally vicious grip, the police officer on my right took his right arm and swung a roundhouse punch and hit me. I was completely in shock. In all my encounters with officials seeking bribes, no one had ever been physical. These men were not only physical, but it had quickly turned vicious. And these were the police! There was no one else to call!!

I could feel my heart plunging into despair. It was worse than fear. Hopelessness was developing, and it was getting worse. The officer on my left began roughing me up as well. Punching and punching. I couldn't believe that this was happening.

I remember thinking, "Lord! I am powerless in this!! AND that guy is walking away with my passport!"

I felt like I was tumbling into a deep black hole. My initial anxiety was plunging into despair, and it was getting worse and worse, degenerating very quickly.

All the while, the two very large and very mean men continued to wail on me, punching me viciously. I lost track of how many blows there were, but each one plunged me further into despair and hopelessness. There was nothing I could do—nothing I could say. I was powerless.

"Deliver me, Lord!" was all I could muster. My hope was gone. I didn't know what would happen, but I thought it would be desperately bad. What made me feel so lost and terrible was the knowledge that I did not have the power to change the situation. I was utterly at the mercy of these tormentors, unless the Lord specifically intervened.

"Lord," I prayed, "You are my only hope. Deliver me, Lord!"

Suddenly, two men broke through the watching crowd. "Stop!" They cried. "This is a man of God! You cannot do this! Release this man of God! We were just with him in Enugu and saw the Lord move mightily. You must release him."

They motioned to the small crowd that had gathered, saying, "Come help this man of God! We cannot allow this. Give him back his passport!"

I suppose that the only part I got right was acting like myself by crying out to the Lord. As ever, He was there with His miraculous presence. He doesn't always make the circumstances resolve like they did in this situation, but He does always offer His presence and His peace.

I was surprised—but obviously thrilled with this development! For not the least reason, the police were totally shocked by the men challenging them, so they stopped punching me.

As I was filled with despair, these two men calling from the crowd gave me what I didn't have on my own—a sense of hope. As the two men who had cried out to help me moved closer, a crowd of people also started to approach; both police officers who were restraining me released their holds on me and looked at the supervisor who held my passport—he was obviously in charge. He looked shocked and took several steps back toward me, paused, and then threw my passport at me. It fluttered to the floor at my feet; then he, and the other officers quickly high-tailed it, disappearing down the corridor of the terminal.

You can only imagine the depth of appreciation I had for the men who had intervened on my behalf! It was a terrible situation in which I lost almost all hope. There was only a shred of hope. I suppose that the only part I got right was acting like myself by crying out to the Lord. As ever, He was there with His miraculous presence. He doesn't always make the circumstances resolve like they did in this situation, but He does always offer His presence and His peace.

The challenge to act like my true self in the midst of despair is that it is a very primal assault at a time when I am very vulnerable. To be able to rally to the cause and stand up rightly, it is necessary to be able to connect with someone else who can encourage me. In this sense, it is not only encouragement in the sense of helping me feel less depressed in the midst of despair, but it can also encourage me, helping me to have the courage to face the situation and act appropriately.

To successfully act like myself in despair, I need a connection with someone else and a positive memory of how things are meant to be, what our values are and how I should be acting if I am being found faithful. When I am in the midst of despair, my first reaction is one of hopelessness. When a supportive person comes, their encouragement can change my perception.

When the Israelites were being oppressed by the Midianites, they cried out for a deliverer. God chose Gideon, but Gideon did not have a deliverer mentality.

> *Now the angel of the LORD came and sat under the oak at Ophrah, which belonged to Joash the Abiezrite, as his son Gideon was beating out wheat in the wine press, to hide it from the Midianites. The angel of the LORD appeared to him and said to him, "The LORD is with you, you mighty warrior." Gideon answered him, "But sir, if the LORD is with us, why then has all this happened to us? (Judges 6:11-13)*

My first reaction may be the same, but the presence of an encourager can strengthen my heart. That's what happened at this airport in Nigeria. In the midst of that encouragement, it is easier for me to stand.

Chapter 17
Acting Like My True Self in SADNESS

Not everyone wants to be healed and whole. Here's how I learned that.

Sixteen weeks into a new church plant, the church planting pastor was removed. I was sent to pick up the pieces. The core group was small and disheartened. There was also a huge "Pastor Wound" with a deep lack of trust toward clergy. I thought I understood how to deal with it because this was my third ministry assignment (in a row!) in which I followed a pastor who had been removed for having an affair. My wife and I *thought* we had a handle on it. Boy, were we wrong!

We had been pursuing family therapy to work through what had happened following the other two errant pastors. The counsel was so valuable, and we were learning so many helpful things, I decided to bring a season of "Family Health" teaching to the church. We introduced wonderful therapists and counselors, and we had weekend retreats and Sunday sermon series about coming to health and maturity.

Although many people flourished and were growing wonderfully, others were restless and increasingly irritable. It was very puzzling until one of the upset people boiled over and shook her finger in my face, saying, "How dare you say that my family and I are not OK!"

Of course, we had not done that at all. We said things like, "Many people find that their families were not able to support them with the love that was needed. Parents who have not experienced love themselves don't know how to give it. God has a plan to address that problem and help each of us get what we need."

As more and more people in the church got increasingly healthy, the ones who refused to admit that they had any issues got increasingly angry. It was a dynamic that was very difficult for me to understand, and it saddened me. I couldn't fathom why people would not want to be healed. Now I understand when people do not have the faith to believe that things can change, it can be too painful for them to face dredging up the disappointments of the past. They would rather keep them buried, hoping that if they don't think about the past, it won't bother them. Of course, that is wrong thinking, but it is the common rationale of people who have been wounded.

In our case, several of the wounded, dysfunctional families banded together to run for leadership positions. They got several seats on the church board and proceeded to oppose everything and to complain vociferously. Maybe you have seen the way antagonists operate. They say things that are nebulous and hard to refute, but they do damage anyway. They say things such as, "Lots of people are upset about lots of things." No specifics. Impossible to refute, but very disruptive, nonetheless.

Then I was presented with a letter demanding my resignation because of a charge of embezzlement. While I was no financial expert, I knew I wasn't stealing, so I asked what was the source of this accusation. They produced photo-copies of checks written to the church but showing that I had deposited them into my personal account. Of course, I had not done that! I couldn't imagine how they had gotten this "evidence." (Later I learned that one of the church members had bragged how she copied the front of one check and the back of another to make it look like I had stolen funds.)

The conflict was severe, but I did not think it was good for anyone to bow to a false accusation, so I refused to resign. My sense of sadness, however, was acute.

The conflict was severe, but I did not think it was good for anyone to bow to a false accusation so I refused to resign. My sense of sadness, however, was acute.

In three churches in a row, we had experienced painful circumstances from another pastor having an affair. Now this fight. I didn't even know how to fight it.

And, I was saddened to think of my grandfather's integrity, and how important it was to him that I be honest. Grandfather had spoken wise words when he told me, "You can't make it through life without experiencing periods of great sadness. Things are often not like the way we would like them to be. Know your duty. Devotion to duty will carry you through times of terrible disquiet."

Also, I was thinking of our Lord and how often He was misunderstood and falsely accused...could I be as faithful as He? I tried to apply His promise of presence with me, for I truly was confident that I had been discipling these people:

> "Go therefore and make disciples of all nations, baptizing them in the name of the Father and of the Son and of the

Holy Spirit, teaching them to observe all things that I have commanded you; <u>and lo, I am with you always, even to the end of the age.</u>" (Matthew 28:19-20; emphasis added)

My wife, Susan, and I sat at home feeling horrible, the sadness overwhelming us. Again and again, we had been plunged into conflict that was not of our making. After being beaten up in other churches by parishioners angry with my predecessors who had betrayed them, we couldn't believe that we were being plunged into conflict again. It seemed so unfair, and yet I had been given important wisdom from my Grandfather, who had once said, "You can't make it through life wihtout experiencing periods of great sadness. Things are often not like the way we would like them to be. Know your duty. Devotion to duty will carry you through times of terrible disquiet."

As we sat numb with pain, we were surprised to hear the doorbell. I went to the door and saw dozens of people at the door and in the front lawn. I could see from their faces that they were not at the door to attack us, so we went out to talk with them.

One of the men who had been pretty lazy about church attendance said, "We all got anonymous mail delivered to our houses today accusing you of embezzling. First of all, it was anonymous. That is suspicious to begin with, but reading the letter, we didn't believe it. Look, we've seen you leave the offering plates on the altar when there was not someone to take it to count. We know you refuse to sign checks. We don't believe it! We made some calls and wanted to come over to encourage you and Susan."

> You can't make it through life without experiencing periods of great sadness. Things are often not like the way we would like them to be. Know your duty. Devotion to duty will carry you through times of terrible disquiet.
>
> -- Brig. Gen. James A. Pickering

Remember that at this time, I didn't know about the photocopied false evidence. I didn't know what charges they could have. In fact, not being a financial expert, I wondered if I had done something unintentionally that was out of bounds.

"What if I've made some kind of financial mistake? I haven't been stealing, but these things are complex. What if there is something technically wrong?"

"Look," said the guy who had taken the lead as spokesperson. "You weren't called as a CPA. You were called to preach. We think you are doing a great job at that."

It is impossible to convey the balm that comment was to my wounded heart. Tears rolled down my cheeks.

The next day was Sunday. I looked out and saw a small group of scowling faces in the front row holding stacks of paper and, I was sure, looking for a fight at the service. With the encouragement of the group that had come to offer their support, the wisdom my grandfather had conveyed to me so much earlier in life, and the confidence in the faithfulness of our Lord Jesus, I knew what to do.

Standing at the front of the church, I said, "Most of you have received anonymous information alleging I have committed financial irregularities. I have signed authorizations for independent audits of all the church accounts as well as all my personal accounts. The auditor will have access to everything. Once that is complete, it should give a financial picture of all the finances. I'm sure some of you would like to do something immediately, but without that independent information, it is not possible to do anything constructive."

Of course, my wife's support was crucial for me, but she was feeling assaulted as well. Thinking back, what really made the difference was the guy in my front yard who saw the mess and made it clear he (and all the others with him) was standing with us. Their action brought a reservoir of hope and encouragement that helped me stand up and "act like my true self."

Chapter 18
Acting Like My True Self in **ANGER**

I didn't have to wonder who it was. I knew it was the Bishop's secretary. She was calling to tell me to come to the Bishop's office at 9:00 o'clock.

I was serving in a tough church—a "pastor eater" they called it because of the way the members of the congregation treated clergy. It had happened many times before. People in the church would call the Bishop Sunday night with their complaints about what they saw as my latest "crime." He was a very "conflict-averse" person, so he would not seek to actually resolve anything. Each time I had a conflict that involved something the Bishop had told me to do, he would call me into the office and give me a list of orders to follow.

The Monday morning drives to the Bishop's office made me sad. I was sad that I had to go through this, but as it carried on for a long time, it also made me angry. The Bishop was putting me in more and more awkward positions and not taking responsibility. I was angry that this particular church where I served as Senior Pastor had almost three hundred years of history, and most of it was filled with conflict. Also, for a pastor with tenure (which I was), what the Bishop was doing was beyond the scope of his authority. Because I was the Senior Pastor (Rector), all the demands he was making actually were under my direct authority with regard to the calling I had to be in charge of the congregation, and they were not part of his area of authority. However, because of my background and the understanding of authority I had gained from my Grandfather, I had a very high view of obeying. The Bishop would give me a list of demands, and I would always comply.

Many times over several years, I was called to the office downtown. I would get my instructions and then head back across the bridge to my home and parish. It was hard doing the things that he had me doing. What was especially irritating was that he would always say, "This is what you have to do, but to protect the office of Bishop, you cannot tell anyone that I have ordered you to do this." What angered me was the fact that he was not really focused on protecting the office of Bishop. He just did not want to take responsibility for his actions! He wanted to act in the dark, and he was perfectly willing for me to pay the price of any conflict.

In obedience to these Bishop's instructions, I never told people that I was being ordered to do this or that. It was also maddening that his instructions were not always the best. Often, they actually would inflame the situation or relationship. Of course, I would get the flack and the blame because I couldn't in good conscience say that the Bishop had ordered something.

Over the years, the corporate identity that had formed in my life was about "my people" being people of integrity and order. That had been writ large by my grandfather. Sadly, I hadn't always been faithful to that vision, but I really wanted to be. When I fell short, I would repent and return to the Lord. I was even pretty good about going to other people and apologizing when I had done something that upset someone.

On this particular day, as I drove across the high ark of the river bridge going to the Bishop's office, my sadness turned to anger. I just wanted this madness to stop!

I knew, however, that there was no future in maintaining anger. I was reminded of my grandfather's council to keep a cool head in conflict. That reminder settled my heart. Then I had to process and release things to get my attitude in the right place so that I could make the commitment to pursue the Bishop's instructions with a glad heart and try to make the best of what he was going to tell me to do.

I knew that this was a crucible season. Circumstances which are out of order and unfair are awful to endure, but they are actually friendly to us. It is what St. Paul wrote in Romans:

> "...And not only that, but we also glory in tribulations, knowing that tribulation produces perseverance; and perseverance, character; and character, hope" (Romans 5:3-4).

Tribulations are not fun, but they bear fruit in us.

This Bishop had a reputation as an evangelical, so I had expected that he would have been supportive because so many people were coming to faith. Over the years, I prayed with four or five hundred people to make first-time commitments to Christ. Many others deepened their faith. In some ways, it was an absolutely glorious season of ministry. At the same time, the church grew amazingly, but the anger and vitriol of the historically rooted people were impossible to overstate. It was not until years later that I would come to understand the dynamic. What was happening was that the influx of newcomers into the community raised property values. When the property values went up, the taxes also went up. Families that had owned plantations since the time of King George before the Revolutionary War were having to sell off acreage from the land that had been owned for generations of their family in order to pay taxes. While I thought that they should be thrilled to see the church growing dramatically, they were deeply upset because they saw growth as the death of their way of life. I was the agent of that death.

I learned that the bishop had a daughter who had been been challenged to commit her life to Christ. She had taken offense and had never set foot back in church. He viewed any upset on the part of people extremely seriously because it was so close to home, especially when someone would complain that they didn't want or need to make a personal commitment to Christ. In their eyes, their institutional and historic connection was adequate.

> The hazing at West Point was terrible. If they really wanted to punish a plebe, they would pour molasses in his hair and tie him to an ant hill. The only way to get through something like that is to focus on the thing that you want more than getting hurt.
>
> -- Brig. Gen. James A. Pickering

On this occasion in the Bishop's office, I had the sense that something was different. I didn't know what to expect, but I did have in my reservoir of wisdom from my grandfather his advice on what to do to keep focused on what is right.

He had told me that "The hazing at West Point was terrible. If they really wanted to punish a plebe, they would pour molasses in his hair and tie him to an ant hill. The only way to get through something like that is to focus on the thing that you want more than getting."

After some trivial conversation, the Bishop said to me, "I'm not going to censor your preaching, but I am directing you that when you are talking with people outside church services, you are no longer allowed to challenge anyone to commit their life to Christ. It is the Holy Spirit's job to bring people to faith, not yours."

I was really angry, but I laughed. I knew it was critically important to be faithful to Jesus. It was important enough to do so even in the face of this Bishop's wrath.

He looked shocked and said, "For years despite all the trouble you have given me, every time I have given you an instruction you have obeyed it. I have checked. People have reported that you have done what I told you to do and appeared to do it with a glad attitude. The only positive constant is that you have always submitted to my authority. Now your laugh tells me that you are not going to obey. Do you mind telling me why?"

"Because," I replied, "You are only a Bishop. You can't overturn the direct command of Jesus Christ. I understand that you will do what you think you have to do to come against me. I will have to live with that. What I won't do is directly disobey Jesus."

The deep roots of my grandfather's call to me of Duty, Honor, and Country played out for me that day in the realization that I had to obey the Lord. If those in temporal authority over me took action against me, so be it, but my commitment to Christ and my understanding of Who I am in Christ meant that to be faithful, I had to "act like myself" and stand up to the Bishop's directive I had just been given.

How things played out after that conversation is actually not the most important thing. The circumstances were just that, circumstances. The motivating principles behind my decision and actions were the important factors.

When faced with having to disobey temporal authority in order to be obedient to Jesus Christ, we really have no choice.

Chapter 19
Acting Like My True Self in SHAME

Sunday morning before church, I stopped by the office to look at my mail. There on top of the file was a signature-required delivery. Someone had signed for it and left it for me. When I saw it was from Pasadena, California, I smiled. I had been traveling there to Fuller Seminary pursuing a Doctorate. It was an amazing program, and I loved going out there to attend classes.

"This should be something good," I mused, but then noticed that it said Municipal Court, Pasadena, California. A stab of fear grabbed me. Not that I was a criminal fugitive, but I couldn't imagine a circumstance in which it would be good to hear from the Court!

I tore open the certified letter and read, "Warrant for Arrest for Failure to Appear." Reading further, I saw that I had missed a court date, and, as a result, the judge had issued a warrant. I felt sick—like a wave of nausea was hitting me. I felt a catch in my throat and a stab of nervous fear. Arrest!!

Some months before, I had gotten a ticket for making a U-turn (one that was legal in the state where I lived, but apparently had not been legal in California!). I had requested, and been granted, an opportunity to attend a one-day traffic school to satisfy the ticket and had mailed the paperwork to California. Somehow, it seemed that the paperwork had not made it to the judge. He was obviously unhappy. To make matters worse, immediately after church services, I was scheduled to fly back to California for my next doctoral class. Barely able to contain my anxiety, I began to wonder if I would be arrested when I got off the plane.

One of my parishioners was walking by the office on his way to the service. I called him over. He was a judge. He would certainly know what to do, but it was humiliating to share with him what was going on.

"Judge, I got a ticket three months ago in Pasadena for making a U-turn. I did the traffic school and sent the paperwork in, but I just got an arrest warrant in the mail! I'm supposed to fly to California tonight. What does this mean? Will they be waiting for me when I get off the plane? Will I even be able to pick up a rental car?"

He laughed, "No. These things happen all the time. Just don't drive like a maniac. Let me see the paperwork…OK. Look, the second page says you have another appearance scheduled for tomorrow at 10:00 am. I *highly* suggest you make that court appearance! If you like, I can put in a call to the judge tomorrow, but I think you will be fine if you just show up on time."

"Thanks, Judge. This is terrible. It's humiliating. I just feel awful." I'm sure I had a downcast hang-dog expression, and I know my ears felt like they were burning hot and I would have bet they were bright red.

> When you've gotten something wrong, remember whom I've taught you you are. The failures don't define you. What defines you is your commitment to stay the course. Be true to that and your feelings will eventually catch up.
>
> -- Brig. Gen. James A. Pickering

"Don't worry, Pastor. I don't think any less of you." What amazing balm that was. I felt like I was at my worst, and he was still glad to be with me!

I had plenty of shame even though he was being kind. I didn't want to risk telling anyone else, though—they might not react as well!

I was nervous on the flight to Los Angeles, and I kept thinking of my Grandfather's words about what to do in a circumstance like this one. He had made it clear that, "When you've gotten something wrong, remember who I've taught you you are. The failures don't define you. What defines you is your commitment to stay the course. Be true to that and your feelings will eventually catch up."

When I arrived, I got a rental car and headed to Pasadena late that night. The next morning, I headed to class. The seminary was only a few blocks away from the Municipal Court, so I figured that I could start class and then slip out in time for my 10:00 appearance.

The class was being taught by Dr. Peter Wagner, a fun-loving professor who had been a missionary for years. Now he was an expert in helping churches and communities prosper and develop and was turning his skills to sharing information—and very corny jokes—with others. Every class started with him telling absolutely lame jokes that were hilarious nonetheless, not for their content, but for the fact that he would get tickled at himself telling the story and start laughing so uproariously he could hardly finish!

Another thing about him was that he was fascinated by prayer. Anytime he heard about a prayer need, he would pull out a 3 x 5 card and write down the need. Later, he would compile a list so he could enter the answers to prayers.

Just before class started, I went up to him to tell him I had to leave about 9:45 am to get to court. Embarrassed, I recounted the story. He said it would be fine to leave, but I could tell he was thinking of something. About an hour later, I got up to walk over to the courthouse and started to slip out of the classroom.

"Wait!" cried Dr. Wagner. "Bill has to go to court to clear up an arrest warrant. We must all stop and pray!"

He pulled out one of his 3 x 5 cards and wrote down the need.

"Some of you gather around. Let's lay hands on him and pray!"

So much for a discrete departure! He recounted all the humiliating details of my predicament. I felt like I wanted to turn into a puddle on the floor. I could feel the shame rising. It was even worse than it had been before! I just wanted it to end so I could slink out of the classroom.

Instead of winding down, Peter was just winding up. He prayed energetically, "Lord Jesus, this is an unjust situation. There should not be an arrest warrant! Your son Bill did everything he was supposed to and now he is being falsely accused. VINDICATE HIM, LORD!"

Oh, my goodness, I didn't know what to think. Then he went on praying with even more fervency, "Vindicate him, Lord. Not only that. Make this whole thing go away! Expunge this from his record. Not only that, Lord, we earnestly pray that the judge will not only release him but will apologize to him!"

"What??" I thought. I knew Peter was larger than life, but I thought he had gone too far with that prayer? Who had heard of a judge *ever* apologizing!

I'm sure I put an embarrassed weak smile on my face and hurried to get out of the classroom as quickly as I could. I can tell you that it was not with abundance of faith. At that moment, I had absolutely no faith. Vindicated? Get an apology? Not likely!

The more I thought about it, the more I realized that Peter had been motivated by goodwill, but I just didn't think that his prayer could be answered affirmatively!

I slipped into the courtroom, where a very angry judge began calling people up.

"You again!" he said to a young man about twenty. Speeding through a school zone. I've seen you before. $1200 fine!" and slammed down his gavel.

"How do you plead to this speeding ticket?" he growled to another person. "Not guilty, your honor."

"Officer, did you observe this gentleman speeding?"

"Yes, your honor," replied the police officer. "I clocked him going 82 in a 55 zone."

"Guilty!" cried the judge. "$575 for the speeding fine, but you also have 16 unpaid parking tickets. Bailiff, take him away. If he doesn't pay every one of them, put him in lockup, and we'll see if anyone loves him. Nobody here does!"

As case after case came before him, they went from bad to worse. The little relief I had felt at Peter's prayer in the classroom was obliterated. I could feel the shame rising up to stratospheric levels.

Then he called my name. "Mr. Atwood! How do you plead? A traffic citation and failure to appear. How do you plead?"

I didn't know what else to do. I had been sitting and praying, trying to calm myself from the anxiety of not knowing what would come, but also from the shame of being there as a wanted fugitive! I knew I had made a mistake, but I also knew that something had gone awry with the paperwork. My grandfather's counsel gave me confidence to speak frankly to the judge:

"When you've gotten something wrong, remember who I've taught you you are. The failures don't define you. What defines you is your commitment to stay the course. Be true to that and your feelings will eventually catch up."

Now when the hour had come, I said, "Guilty, your honor, but with an explanation if you will allow it."

"Go ahead, Mr. Atwood. Go ahead."

I was standing. It took all the fortitude I could muster to stand and face him and try to speak without my voice squeaking! Somehow, I managed.

"Your honor, several months ago I did make what was an illegal U-turn here in Pasadena, though it would have been legal where I live. I asked for, and was granted, the opportunity to do a traffic school course to satisfy the ticket. I took that course and mailed it to the court. Then yesterday, I received a certified letter in Florida where I live with an arrest warrant for Failure to Appear. I had no idea I was supposed to appear. I thought when I sent in the traffic school certificate the matter was settled."

I didn't know how he was going to receive that information, but it felt good to stand up for myself. Although I was afraid that he was about to lower the boom on me, for a moment, I felt peaceful and strong.

"Bailiff!" cried the judge at the top of his lungs. "Get in here!" A clerk ran to the adjacent office and dragged the bailiff into the courtroom.

"Listen," grumbled the judge, "This gentleman has flown across the country to appear in this courtroom. This paperwork doesn't have a time-stamp. Bailiff, I am sick and tired of you messing up paperwork. I'm putting you on notice that if this happens again, I'm going to lock you up for 30 days for contempt. Do you understand??!!??"

> *I didn't know how he was going to receive that information, but it felt good to stand up for myself. Although I was afraid that he was about to lower the boom on me, for a moment, I felt peaceful and strong.*

Then he turned to me as I was standing open-mouthed staring at him. "See this paperwork? This incomplete mishandled paperwork that forced you to cross the entire country to appear? Watch this!!" With that he took my file and ripped it in half and then in half again and again, and threw it up in the air. "How about that?" he exclaimed. "No more paperwork. No file. No charges. No warrant!"

I was dumbfounded watching as the confetti made from my ticket and paperwork fluttered around the judge's bench. I just stood silently wondering what was next.

"Mr. Atwood, I would say you are free to go, but there is one more thing. This court and the people of Pasadena would like to apologize for the terrible unfair way that you were treated. That should never have happened. On behalf of a system that let you down, I apologize. You are free to go."

It was almost unbelievable. Not only had every facet of Peter's prayer been answered about not having to pay a fine, and having my ticket dismissed, but just as he had prophetically prayed, I was actually leaving the court *with an apology*. What's amazing is that it came without an ounce of faith on my part. I never thought there would be an apology! And, yet God has promised,

> *"Call upon me, and I will answer you, and show you great and mighty things, which you do not know." (Jeremiah 33:33)*

Thinking back on my part, the only encouragement I had was the fact that I was able to stand up in the midst of shame and speak my mind to the judge. I knew that I had "acted like myself" in being bold, yet honest and respectful. I certainly never imagined things would play out the way they did, but I'm certainly glad that they did. I'm also thrilled that Peter Wagner's prayer and faith exceeded mine! At least I was able to take comfort from being able to stand up for myself with the judge in the midst of the shame of the ticket and the arrest warrant. Without a doubt, the connection with my friend the judge at home, and the support from Peter and my classmates had been amazing.

Now, imagine what happened when I got back to the class filled with fifty doctoral students and reported that my name was cleared, and my record expunged. I will confess that I paused for dramatic effect, and then said, "It culminated with the judge tearing up my paperwork into tiny pieces, throwing it into the air, dismissing the case, and then—wait for it—he apologized for the terrible treatment I had received! The classroom erupted into cheers and applause with everyone on their feet. Amazing.

When we are shamed or feeling shame for some behavior, we have the Scriptures to help us get a better perspective and to address the situation properly. If, like David, we have truly sinned and our shame is warranted, we can turn to Psalm 51:1-4 for guidance and help. We also know that Jesus Christ bore our sins and our iniquities, and we have the confidence that when we confess our sins, God is "faithful and just to forgive us our sins and to cleanse us of all unrighteousness."

Chapter 20
Acting Like My True Self in DISGUST

Noah was a Kurd. Kurdistan is where the Israelites were taken in the Babylonian captivity. For thousands of years, the Kurds have had a robust presence in kind of a circle that stretches across northern Iraq, eastern Syria, Southern Turkey, southwestern Azerbaijan, and western Iran. The Kurdish area in northern Iraq has been a semi-autonomous region they call Kurdistan, where the Kurds were left (somewhat) alone to govern themselves.

I had friends in Kurdistan drilling water wells to replace ones that Sadaam Hussein had poisoned. (He hated the Kurd's independent streak!) My friends were quietly doing evangelism but used the well drilling to open doors. They had invited me to come to teach how to do evangelism using home cell groups because it was not possible to plant new churches.

Unemployment in Kurdish, northern Iraq, hovered around 90 percent, with the only jobs being taxi drivers and private security forces. The area had formerly been extremely prosperous, with educated people, beautiful homes, and lovely cars. Oppression from Sadaam had crashed the economy and left schools closed and pretty much all church services obliterated. There were no police, fire, or mail delivery personnel. Electricity ran for only a few hours a week. Tap water was very unreliable, and not clean when running.

Kurds are extremely social. I visited one chief's home where he told me that he had been quite prosperous, paying for his children to attend western universities, and paying cash for the two Volvo sedans in his garage.

"Look at that wall. Do you notice anything unusual about it?" asked my host.

"Not really. It just looks like a wall."

"Look how thick it is," he said.

I could see that it was more than a foot thick. Looking at a window, it was easy to see how unusual it was once he had pointed it out. "What's that about? Were you building a fortress?"

"No," he replied. "It was my bank. Those walls are hollow and are completely filled with cash. Sadly, Sadaam outlawed the money we had and now it is worthless! It was worth hundreds of thousands of U.S. dollars. Now it's totally worthless!"

I was amazed at the calm that he exhibited after having lost so much, but this seemed to be common among the Kurds. They have an immense ability to endure suffering. Maybe it was their heritage going back to the time of Daniel and the Babylonian captivity!

Kurdish Mastau

My friend who lived there doing the water wells leaned over and whispered to me, "He likes you. Kurds don't share personal information with others unless they really trust them. He is treating you like a chief. For dignitaries, t have a welcome ceremony. They are probably about to bring out the *Mastau*."

While the Kurds were busy talking among themselves, my friend went on, "*Mastau* is a vile drink. It's made up of buttermilk, yogurt, salt, and vinegar. They serve it to guests they want to honor. Here's the deal...you have to drink it down in one go. It is a huge offense not to finish it. Also, you can't sip it. The only acceptable way is gulping it down. Good luck!"

Goodness, this sounded disgusting. Even worse was the prospect of a terrible cultural faux pas that would undermine the Gospel work among these people.

My grandfather had an answer to that one, too. He had once said to me, "I love coconut cake. I love everything about it. I like the taste, the texture, and the smell. I also like remembering the celebration when we have it. Remembering coconut cake helps me make it through difficult times." Coconut cake sounded so much better than mastau!

> I love coconut cake. I love everthing about it. I like the taste, the texture, and the smell. I also like remembering the celebration when we have it. Remembering coconut cake helps me make it through difficult times.
> -- Gen. James A. Pickering

My thoughts were brought back to the present and the impending assault of Mastau by the arrival of the chief's wife coming into the parlor with a tray of glasses filled with a questionable looking whitish goo. The Kurd's lit up with joy. They obviously loved this *"Mastau"* stuff. Coming to me with the tray, Mrs. Chief motioned to me to take one of the glasses. I could see the others holding their full glasses at the ready, just about to drink theirs down. My eye caught the eye of my friend who was seated nearby, the one who had warned me about *Mastau*. I took great comfort from him. Somehow, his comradeship, encouraged and strengthened me. The power of community can even be stronger than the negative power of disgust!

I was earnestly praying, "Help me, Lord. Don't let me choke or throw this up and cause an international incident!"

The chief was giving a speech, but I didn't really listen. First of all, it was in the local Sorani dialect. Secondly, I was fixating on the drink in my hand. Even at arm's length I could smell the buttermilk and vinegar. Seriously, would it be possible to design anything more disgusting? It just reeked. I could feel my stomach churning, and I hadn't even consumed any of the vile swill yet!

> *Even at arm's length I could smell the buttermilk and vinegar. Seriously, would it be possible to design anything more disgusting? It just reeked. I could feel my stomach churning, and I hadn't even consumed any of the vile swill yet!*

My stomach was doing the kind of constricting contractions like you get just before vomiting. This was terrible! I remembered Judith Viorst's children's book, *Alexander and the Terrible, Horrible, No Good, Very Bad Day*, "I think I'll move to Australia." But Australia was not in the works this day. *Mastau* was!

I could tell that the chief's speech was winding down, and it would soon be the moment of truth. I could feel a bead of sweat on my forehead. My nose was reacting oddly to the complex mixture of smells coming from the glass. I remembered my grandfather's words about focusing on something pleasant when having to endure something difficult: "I love coconut cake. I love everything about it. I like the taste, the texture, and the smell. I also like remembering the celebration when we have it. Remembering coconut cake helps me make it through difficult times."

With a twinkle in his eye, the chief offered the equivalent of, "Ready, Set, Go!" in Kurdish Sorani. Every person in the room was looking at the American, waiting to see if I would embarrass myself.

The room suddenly seemed hot, but the glass was cold in my hand. I was visualizing buttermilk, salt and vinegar—it seemed in equal proportions! Mixed in as well was yogurt. Not the fluffy western kind from Yoplait, but the pungent plain kind that had probably fermented on the counter for a couple decades before serving it today. I hadn't even tasted it yet, but my stomach was starting to churn.

I saw Kurdish heads throw back and begin to glug the noxious stuff down. I wasn't able to put it off any longer, so I tipped the glass to my lips with an urgent prayer, "Help me, Lord. Don't let this come right back up!"

My stomach knotted as I began to drink, and began to feel the constricting spasms in my gut that precede vomiting. I figured my best chance at getting this done was just to swill it down... it was awful. Disgusting. What kind of eccentric culture would conceive of something like this horrific drink—and call it hospitality!

My stomach churned, but I bravely put on my, "You Kurdish guys really know how to party and make a guy feel welcome" face.

With a final gurgle, I finished the disgusting glass. There was a churn in my stomach, but then it began to still. For the first time since this whole *Mastau* debacle surfaced, there was a thread of hope that I was going to survive it, without leaving ignominy and failure—not to mention the other contents of my stomach—all over the floor. I had not even considered that His promise would apply to something like this, yet He is faithful and He has promised that I, like Paul, "can do all things through Christ who strengthens me" (Philippians 4:13).

My face wore a subtle, gracious smile, and my heart was at rest. I had survived what is arguably the worst substance on earth to be ritually consumed, except perhaps century-old Chinese duck eg;s, buried nine months in the ground Korean kimchi;, or Nigerian melon seed soup, which has a half an inch layer of grease floating on its surface. (Just to spice things up, the Nigerians also toss a vegetable into the soup that tastes like tobacco. Yum.)Mastau stands with honor in this Hall of Fame of Disgust.

The heart of disgust is the knowledge that something is not "life-giving." In spite of the noxious experience of having to slug down the *Mastau*, I had prevailed. I had called upon the Lord, and He had answered me! I had successfully "acted like my true self"—and avoided a cross-cultural train wreck.

Chapter 21
Acting Like My True Self In FEAR

The aging Russian bus with my Air force crew and me rattled past scores of identical run-down, gray high-rise buildings, all filled with identical flats for workers. We were traveling through the streets of Simferopol, Ukraine, to a hotel on the way from the airport. We rode under the ever watchful gaze of our translator and driver. Along the way, we passed sign after sign emblazoned with Cyrillic characters of the Russian language. Having come to fly The White House staff and Secret Service members who accompanied the President to a summit at Yalta, we were headed to the hotel.

As I looked at the signs, I could see that the letters were a combination of English and Greek letters, plus a few squiggles for a couple of weird letters. Having studied Greek, I was able to sound out a surprising number of words I could recognize. Passing what looked to be a movie theater, I saw the sign that said театр космос. Pronouncing the combination of letters I said, "Look. That's The Cosmos Theater."

Immediately, the lady who was assigned as our translator jumped from her seat at the front of the bus and raced back to me, putting her face in front of mine. Very agitated, she said, "How did you read that sign? You wrote on your entry form that no one on the crew could speak or read Russian. How did you read it?"

I replied, "It was just a combination of Greek and English letters. Really simple actually."

Not satisfied, she demanded, "Why do you know Greek?"

With the USSR's hostility to faith, I could feel my body tense up and I sensed danger. I thought of all the stories I had heard about the courage of Brother Andrew, who had devoted his life to smuggling Bibles into Russia and other parts of the Soviet Union. There was a constriction in my throat. I recognized that it might be awkward — terrible even — if the tracts and Christian material in my suitcase were discovered. Nevertheless, I replied, "I have studied Greek to be able to read the Bible better."

Her eyes opened wide and her mouth fell open. She quickly glanced over her shoulder to see if the driver was watching us, or paying attention to the traffic. Happily, he seemed absorbed in steering his way through all the vehicles around us on Simferopol's streets.

She leaned over close to me putting her mouth next to my ear. I was straining to listen over the street noise and the rumbles of our bus. I could feel the buzz in my abdomen of excitement and awareness of danger. Waiting, I was expecting her to say something derisive about religion following the communist line, but to my utter amazement, I heard her speak in very low tones. It was as quiet as a whisper but actually spoken very deliberately in marked, measured tones, "I have read the *Cross and the Switchblade.*"

Rather than speaking derisively about faith, I knew she was telling me she was a Christian!

I started to reply but she touched her lips and shook her head toward the driver. "They are always listening." From that moment, we looked for an opportunity to speak, but everywhere we went, there was always someone else there listening. There was a heightened sense of tension—constantly looking for the chance to speak. For several days, we went through the careful tension of wanting to find the chance to talk, but we had to hold back because of the danger of spies listening to everything. Finally on our last day, we were together on my plane. I was getting ready to fly back to the States. The Secret Service agents and White House staff were on their way but hadn't arrived yet. Suddenly, I realized we were alone on the plane. It was the only place where I could be sure there were no microphones. We had closed the aircraft and sealed it with "boxcar seals" to insure that no one had entered the plane or tampered with it.

> From the General:
> (When I graduated from USAF Pilot Training)
> I want you to have my service automatic 1911 Colt .45 pistol. I got it when I graduated from West Point in 1916 and carried it through the battle of Château Thirey in WW I and the Battle of the Bulge in WW II.
> You need it. Remember. There are bad people out there.
>   -- Brig. Gen. James A. Pickering

Excited, with my heart now pounding, I turned to her and said, "I've been wanting to talk with you. I was amazed to hear what you said on the bus. I took it to mean you are a Christian."

"Yes," she replied, "but I must walk very carefully. For my job, I have to be a member of the Communist Party. To be identified as a Christian would mean immediate arrest. If they found me with a Bible, they would send me to a Gulag for possession of pornography!"

That was awful. In addition, I was really disappointed because I had Bibles and Christian materials in my suitcase that I was going to offer her. Now I realized that was not possible. We spoke about her secret fellowship of believers. It was painful to hear and sobering, but there was an undercurrent of joy that the Gospel was present and growing even in the midst of such oppression.

"Hey!" I exclaimed. "I have an idea. Would it work if I gave you my Prayer Book? It has tons of scripture in it—all the Gospels and Psalms, and lots of other Bible passages as well. Could I leave that with you?"

"Hmmm," she mused. I could tell she was thinking. "I think so. I could probably get away with a personal memento. I think it could be OK."

I moved over to where my bags were and I reached in to get the Prayer Book. She followed over to that side of the plane.

"You know we pray for you. Not by name of course. I didn't know your name until this week. But we pray for the Christians in the easy parts of the world. We pray for the church to undergo persecution so that your faith will be strong and pure."

I felt a stab of fear at that. It was like something very cold and metallic in the pit of my stomach. I didn't know what to say. It didn't seem right to say, "Thank you," so I just said, "Oh. I see."

Pulling my bright red leather Prayer Book out of my suitcase I turned and handed it to her. My eye caught the glint of my name in gold on the cover. I thought, "Oh, great. Now will they pray for me by name to undergo persecution?"

At the exact moment I handed it to her, the KGB secret police came up the steps into the plane. The stab of fear I felt was magnified a thousand times. It took my breath away, and I could feel my palms being sweaty and my heart racing.

I didn't know what to do. I was at a total loss. Here right in front of the KGB, I had given her a Christian Prayer Book filled with Scripture. Not only that, it was bright red leather and had my name stamped on the cover in gold. Hard to miss! I wish I could say that I had a plan or a response, but I was just startled and frozen. Not so my friend. She was ready in all seasons!

Turning to the KGB agents, instead of trying to hide the Prayer Book, she held it up in front of them. "Look!" She said. This American pilot has had such a wonderful time here in Ukraine, he has just given me a personal memento from his childhood. It's something really important to him and he wanted to share it with me!"

The KGB agents were a bit startled, but it was more awe than shock. The one who was the obvious leader came over close to me, invading my personal space. Through my interpreter, he said, "How wonderful that you have enjoyed your time here. We are very pleased. It is also wonderful that you have given this important memento from your childhood to your interpreter. That is a very important and grand gesture! We must give you something of great importance as a symbol of our friendship and your visit here!"

At that, he reached onto the lapel of his suit coat and unpinned a medal. I recognized it. This was a really big deal.

"You have given a prized possession. In return, this is *my* most prized possession. It is my Order of Lenin, given to me for my service to the motherland." At that, he took the medal and pinned it to my shirt, and gave me huge kisses, one on each cheek. Very Russian!

Everyone was emotional, but I for different reasons. I was moved because although I had choked and had no idea how to handle the situation, my translator had known and had reacted very well. She demonstrated amazing calm in the face of the surprise arrival of the KGB. She was able to be faithful to her true identity and stand up courageously in the face of great danger. I was a bystander to her calm and courage, but I learned from it just the same.

> *Everyone was emotional, but I for different reasons. I was moved because although I had choked and had no idea how to handle the situation, my translator had known and had reacted very well.*

The profundity of the situation struck me. Here in the midst of great danger, my new Christian friend had been able to maintain such calm in the midst of a great storm that peace spread to the rest of us. Her clever response to the KGB surprise was totally authentic, completely true, and also the perfect action to rescue us. In addition, what had just happened was a Communist Medal—the Order of Lenin—was just effectively traded for a book filled with Scripture, right under the noses of the KGB. What an amazing thing!!

I learned a lot about how big God is, and how He is willing to help us in the midst of trials. Whereas I had not rallied to the event, my translator friend had. It really showed me the truth of the Scripture where Jesus shared:

> *"Now when they bring you to the synagogues and magistrates and authorities, do not worry about how or what you should answer, or what you should say. For the Holy Spirit will teach you in that very hour what you ought to say." (Luke 12:11-12)*

In this case, I had failed to act like my true self, but my friend had succeeded. She had learned from years of being at the ready. Not only did she rescue us from the danger at hand, she schooled me in having a better understanding of the Kingdom, a better understanding of myself, and a better appreciation for being ready. What she modeled for me was a pathway of processing fear in a much better way. Now that I had seen it in the middle of a firestorm, it had a huge impact on my thinking for future conflicts.

Chapter 22
Connections & Community

As you have read stories about returning to joy and acting like myself, I hope you have noticed how important relationships are to the process. Belonging is absolutely essential to thriving. In *Joy Starts Here*, Wilder, Khouri, Coursey, and Sutton write:

> When we create belonging, our joy extends an invitation for others to grow joy together with us. Joyful belonging grows relationships, seeks others and builds when others smile back. Creating belonging is the best indicator of maturity at any age. When we create belonging around us, we are growing a network of joyful relationships. Our "herd is connected and empowered by joy and seeks to invite others to share joy with us.[33]

As Siegel explains, our connections are not just emotional ones but are actually shared neuro-pathways whereby our minds are linked. Ideally, this process begins when we are very young—infants in fact. By syncing with our parents (principally our mothers initially, and then our fathers) we can begin to learn to return to joy from negative emotions. As I've tried to describe, the process can be a bit different for each of the "big six" negative emotions, but the similarity is that we most readily return to joy when we can share with another person. That is with people first, but the great Person, Jesus Christ, can also be a source of syncing, calming, and recovering joy. Over the years, what I have experienced is the process of returning to joy is most often sparked by human kindness and then deepened by intimate fellowship with the Lord. Now, in most cases, I can return to joy in about a minute or a minute and a half.

As my understanding of Jesus grows, He reveals to me more and more about my True Identity. You can read more about this in Immanuel Journaling/Immanuel Process, etc.[34] As we become more aware of who we truly are, it is increasingly natural to see how that true identity can be manifest. The wonderful truth is that the more we act like our true selves,

---

[33] Wilder EJ, Khouri EM, Coursey CM, Sutton SD. (2014) *Joy Starts Here*. East Peoria, IL: Shepherd's House, Inc.

[34] Wilder EJ, Kang A, Loppnow J, Loppnow S. (2015) *Joyful Journey: Listening to Immanuel*. East Peoria, IL: Shepherd's House, Inc., and Lehman K. (2016) *Immanuel Approach for Emotional Healing and For Life*. CA: Immanuel Publishing. http://www.kclehman.com

the more fruit we experience. St. Paul writes:

> *But the fruit of the Spirit is love, joy, peace, longsuffering, kindness, goodness, faithfulness, gentleness, self-control.*
> *(Galatians 5:22-23)*

Those are the attitudes that we want in our lives. They come to us most abundantly when we are in a relationship with Jesus, and living in a community of relationships that are rooted in joy.

As you seek to find and build those attitudes in your life, it may be that you are not surrounded by a healthy, mature, joy-filled community. That does not mean that you are just "out of luck." There are many things you can do. In the back of this book is a Bibliography of helpful books. It is expanded to see some videos on YouTube.com.

Another good source of life and growth are the ThriveToday.org week-long tracks. You can read about those events here: https://thrivetoday.org

Journey Groups are online zoom.us small groups whereby you can link with others who want to learn to apply skills to build joy. One of the pastors with whom I work wrote this about his experience of a Journey Group:

"I want to thank you for bringing this whole "brain science" teaching and now the Journey Groups to us. The concepts are so important — how our brains work, how attachments are formed, how identity is shaped. I get those through the books. But the Journey Groups are even more important because in them, I'm able to practice what I'm learning because that is the point... Now, I'm in a Journey Group with two other pastors every week, and we're really connecting to each other as we learn and grow. It's WONDERFUL."[35]

You can sign up for a Journey Group here:
https://deeperwalkinternational.org/journey/
Amy Brown coordinates those groups. She is one of the most knowledgeable people in the world on building community through small groups. Though it is more difficult to establish the connection of two people's Cingulate Cortices when we link with others via electronic means, Amy even shares skills that can multiply the fruit of a video conference.

---

[35] The Rev. Theron Walker, Emmaus Anglican Church, Castle Rock, Colorado.

Deeper Walk International [36] (http://deeperwalkinternational.org)has discipleship resources that can help congregations move toward fulfilling their potential, being the kind of communities that are joy-filled, redemptive, and ones that build maturity.

In any case, I hope that you know you were not meant to be alone, and your inheritance in Jesus Christ is an inheritance of joy. He sśffered, died, rose, and lives today so that your joy might be full. Please don't miss out on what He has for you directly, or through His people!

I hope I will see you along the journey of joy!

---

[36] https://deeperwalkinternational.org

Scriptures for Those Times When Joy Is Interrupted

Despair

Psalm 61:1-3

To the leader: with stringed instruments. Of David.
Hear my cry, O God;
listen to my prayer.
From the end of the earth I call to you,
when my heart is faint.
Lead me to the rock
that is higher than I;
for you are my refuge,
a strong tower against the enemy.

Philippians 4:19

And my God will fully satisfy every need of yours according to his riches in glory in Christ Jesus.

Sadness

Psalm 30:11-12

You have turned my mourning into dancing;
you have taken off my sackcloth
and clothed me with joy,
so that my soul may praise you and not be silent.
O LORD my God, I will give thanks to you forever.

Joel 2:25-27

I will restore to you the years
that the swarming locust has eaten,
the hopper, the destroyer, and the cutter,
my great army, which I sent against you.
You shall eat in plenty and be satisfied,
and praise the name of the LORD your God,
who has dealt wondrously with you.

Anger

Ephesians 4:26-27

Be angry but do not sin; do not let the sun go down on your anger, and do not make room for the devil.

Psalm 91:1

You who live in the shelter of the Most High,
who abide in the shadow of the Almighty,
will say to the LORD, "My refuge and my fortress;
my God, in whom I trust."
For he will deliver you from the snare of the fowler
and from the deadly pestilence;
he will cover you with his pinions,
and under his wings you will find refuge;
His faithfulness is a shield and buckler.
You will not fear the terror of the night,
or the arrow that flies by day,
or the pestilence that stalks in darkness,
or the destruction that wastes at noonday.

Psalm 91:7

A thousand may fall at your side,
ten thousand at your right hand,
but it will not come near you.

Shame

Hebrews 12:2

...looking to Jesus the pioneer and perfecter of our faith, who for the sake of the joy that was set before him endured the cross, disregarding its shame, and has taken his seat at the right hand of the throne of God.

Disgust

John 1:1-4

In the beginning was the Word, and the Word was with God, and the Word was God. He was in the beginning with God. All things were made through Him, and without Him nothing was made that was made. In Him was life, and the life was the light of men.

Fear

Isiah 41:10

Do not fear, for I am with you,
do not be afraid, for I am your God;
I will strengthen you, I will help you,
I will uphold you with my victorious right hand.

Hebrews 13:5b-6

He has said, "I will never leave you or forsake you." So we can say with confidence,"The Lord is my helper; I will not be afraid. What can anyone do to me?"

Psalm 16:11

You show me the path of life.
In your presence there is fullness of joy;
in your right hand are pleasures forevermore.

Notes:

www.ingramcontent.com/pod-product-compliance
Lightning Source LLC
Chambersburg PA
CBHW070852050426
42453CB00012B/2155